AF560754

Gleanings in Ancient Indian Numismatics

Gleanings in Ancient Indian Numismatics

Prashant Srivastava

AGAM KALA PRAKASHAN
DELHI

First Published 2014

ISBN : 978 -81-7320-142-4

Published by:
Dr. Agam Prasad, M.A., Ph.D., Diploma in Museology
For **Agam Kala Prakashan**
34, Central Market, Ashok Vihar
Delhi - 110 052
Tel.: 27212195, 65688806-7
Fax: +91-11-27212195
Email: agambooks@gmail.com, agambook@yahoo.com
www.agamkala.com

Composed by:
Aman Printographics
Delhi - 110 052
Mobile: 9891395309

Printed by:
Chawla Offset Printers
Wazirpur Village, Ashok Vihar
Delhi-110 052

Printed in India

Dedicated to the memory
of my aunt,
Smt Snehlata Srivastava

Contents

Preface

Ancient Indian numismatics has acted as a potent tool in the hands of a historian in his attempt to solve many a problem of ancient Indian history. A K Narain has rightly observed : 'For certain periods (*of ancient Indian history*)[1] the historian has to be a numismatist'.[2] A study of coins has helped determine the family, date, and extent of rule of various rulers; it has assisted in identifying places known from literary and other sources, and locating the habitat of peoples; it has provided insights into the socio-economic dynamics of various periods of ancient Indian history; it has shed welcome light on mytho-religious developments.

But the field of ancient Indian numismatics is, itself, fraught with a number of problems and debates, which make the study of the coins of ancient India, such a rewarding and interesting endeavour. These problems and debates include those of the origin and antiquity of coinage in India; introduction of the die-striking mode of fabrication of coins, and of legends on ancient Indian coins; problems of attribution; of the rarity of busts and of realistic portraiture on ancient Indian coins; and of identification of deities on coins. Then, there are some enigmatic types; the significance of

1 Words in italics, within parenthesis, mine.

2 A K Narain, *The Indo-Greeks*, (Oxford, 1957), p. viii.

monograms appearing on coins; certain coin denominations; and forgery of coins, which pose problems.

I have presented, in a summarized manner, and often through examples, some of these vexing problems of ancient Indian numismatics, which appear to defy solution. Scholars have been endeavouring to find solutions to these problems. I have, myself, devoted over a quarter of a century, pondering over such problems and debates. However, at best, the solutions proposed may be termed as probable, and not final and universally accepted ones.

I wish to put on record my sincere thanks to my teacher, Prof K K Thaplyal, for going through the manuscript, and offering valuable suggestions for the improvement of the monograph. I owe a deep sense of gratitude to my parents, Smt Pushplata Srivastava and Shri Priyonath Srivastava, who have always been a source of strength for me. And a big thankyou to my wife, and daughters—Pratichi and Purvi, for bearing with me.

05 December 2013 **Prashant Srivastava**

List of Illustrations

Coin no.	Details
27	Coin of Antialkidas
28	Coin of Hermaios
29	Coin of Heraos
30	Coin of Hyrkodes
31	Coin of Phseigacharis
32	Coin of V'ima Kadphises
33	Coin of Nahapāna
34	Coin of Nahapāna
35	Coin of Nahapāna
36	Coin of Chashṭana
37	Coin of Rudradāman I
38	Coin of Dāmajadaśrī
39	Coin of Jīvadāman
40	Coin of Rudrasiṁha I
41	Coin of Rudrasena I
42	Coin of Dāmasena
43	Coin of Yajña Sātakarṇi
44	Coin of Yajña Sātakarṇi
45	Silver coin of Chandragupta II
46	Silver coin of Kumāragupta I
47	Silver coin of Kumāragupta I
48	Silver coin of Skandagupta
49	Coin of Traikūṭaka Dahrasena
50	Coin of Traikūṭaka Vyāghrasena
51	Coin of Hermaios + Kalliope
52	Coin of Plato, showing monogram
53	Kushāṇa coin showing monogram
54	Coin of Chandragupta I-Kumāradevī
55	Coin of Chandragupta I-Kumāradevī
56	Coin of Chandragupta I-Kumāradevī
57	Coin of Chandragupta I-Kumāradevī

1

Origin of coinage in India

The various theories proposed by scholars over the years for the origin of Indian coinage are quite well known,[1] and just a brief survey of these theories shall suffice.

H H Wilson suggested that the Indians learnt the art of coinage from the Bactrians and the Romans.[2] James Prinsep, too, feels that there was no coinage in India prior to the advent of Alexander.[3] These two scholars would, thus, place the antiquity of Indian coinage somewhere in the fourth century BC, or even later. Kennedy is of the view that the Indian punch-marked coins were copied from the Babylonian coins

---

1 See D R Bhandarkar, *Carmichael Lectures on Ancient Indian Numismatics*, (reprint, Patna, 1984), pp. 36ff; A S Altekar, Origin and Early History of Coinage in Ancient India, *Journal of the Numismatic Society of India* 15(1), (1953), pp. 1-26.

2 H H Wilson, *Ariana Antiqua—A Descriptive Account of the Antiquities and Coins of Afghanistan*, (reprint, Delhi, 1971), pp. 403-404.

3 James Prinsep, *Journal of the Asiatic Society of Bengal* 1, p. 394; James Prinsep, *Essays on Indian Antiquities, Historic, Numismatic, and Palaeographic* 1, (edited by Edward Thomas, London, 1858), pp. 53-54.

circa sixth century BC,[1] and this seems to have the support of V A Smith, who says that Indian coinage began around the seventh century BC as a result of foreign maritime trade.[2] John Allan believes that the idea of coinage was suggested in India by the Iranian *sigloi*, in the late fifth or early fourth century BC, although the punch-marked coins are entirely different from the Achaemenian coins. He opines that the Nanda rulers of the third quarter of the fourth century BC, who were famous for their great wealth, were, perhaps, the first to issue coins in India.[3] J-A Decourdemanche, too, believes that the punch-marked coins are simply an Indian variety of the coinage of the Achaemenians.[4]

However, there is no such similarity between the punch-marked coins, the earliest available coins of India, and the Greek/Graeco-Bactrian, Babylonian, and Iranian coins, as to warrant that these punch-marked coins were inspired by

1 Kennedy, *Journal of the Royal Asiatic Society of Great Britain and Ireland* 1898, pp. 279ff, *vide* A S Altekar, Origin and Early History of Coinage in Ancient India, *Journal of the Numismatic Society of India* 15(1), (1953), pp. 1-26, on p. 2.

2 V A Smith, *Imperial Gazetteer* 2, p. 183, *vide* A S Altekar, Origin and Early History of Coinage in Ancient India, *Journal of the Numismatic Society of India* 15(1), (1953), pp. 1-26, on p. 2. *Cf* V A Smith, *Coins of Ancient India—Catalogue of the Coins in the Indian Museum, Calcutta, including the Cabinet of the Asiatic Society of Bengal* 1 (reprint, Varanasi, 1972), p. 133, where he places the introduction of coinage in India around 500 BC or 600 BC.

3 John Allan, *Catalogue of the Coins of Ancient India, in the British Museum, London*, (London, 1936), p. lxxi, where he also says that 'there is no evidence that coinage in India is older than the Nanda period'.

4 J-A Decourdemanche, *Note sur Les Anciennes Monnaies de L'Inde Dites 'Punch-Marked' Coins et sur Le Système de Manou, Journal Asiatique*, January-February 1912, pp. 117-132.

them, and, hence, most of the Indian scholars, and a number of European ones, too, do not subscribe to the view that Indian coinage owes its origin to foreigners—Greeks or Bactrians, Babylonians, Iranians. E J Rapson suggests that the punch-marked coins were developed independently of any foreign influence.[1] Edward Thomas states that the '[d]esigns, treatment and die-devices (of ancient Indian coins), evince independent thought.'[2] Cunningham, who places the punch-marked coins as early as 1000 BC, too, does not accept the various theories regarding the foreign origin of Indian coinage.[3] A number of reputed scholars, like D R Bhandarkar,[4] S K Chakrabortty,[5] A S Altekar,[6]

---

1 E J Rapson, *Indian Coins*, (Strassburg, 1897), p. 2; E J Rapson, Counter-marks on Early Persian and Indian Coins, *Journal of the Royal Asiatic Society of Great Britain and Ireland*, 1895, pp. 865-877, on pp. 869ff.

2 Edward Thomas, in James Prinsep, *Essays on Indian Antiquities, Historic, Numismatic, and Palaeographic* 1, (ed Edward Thomas, London, 1858), pp. 211ff; also Edward Thomas, *Ancient Indian Weights*, (London, 1885), p. 34. See A S Altekar, Origin and Early History of Coinage in Ancient India, *Journal of the Numismatic Society of India* 15(1), (1953), pp. 1-26, on pp. 2-3.

3 Alexander Cunningham, *Coins of Ancient India*, (reprint, Varanasi, 1971), p. 43.

4 D R Bhandarkar, *Carmichael Lectures on Ancient Indian Numismatics*, (reprint, Patna, 1984), pp. 37ff.

5 S K Chakrabortty, *A Study of Ancient Indian Numismatics*, (Mymensingh, 1931), pp. 34-36.

6 A S Altekar, Origin and Early History of Coinage in Ancient India, *Journal of the Numismatic Society of India* 15(1), (1953), pp. 1-26, on pp. 1-8.

and others[1] are staunch advocates of the theory of the indigenous origin of Indian coins.

In recent years, the theory of the foreign (Graeco-Iranian) origin of Indian coinage has been revived by scholars like M K Dhavalikar[2] and Joe Cribb.[3] Most of the punch-marked coins are in silver. Dhavalikar expresses surprise over the sudden introduction of a full-fledged silver coinage in India, when all the ancient religious texts refer to the monetary use of gold only. Unstamped bar-shaped silver ingots were used in central Asia, which was under Iranian influence,[4] and Dhavalikar suggests that the origin of the Indian bent bars may be traced to this Iranian practice.[5]

Joe Cribb's theory may be summed up as follows[6] : The cup-shaped coins (coins no. 1-4) and the early series of regular punch-marked coins share 'characteristics of design and technology', and as there is no evidence to show that the latter were the precursor of the former, the early series of

---

1 P L Gupta, *Coins*, (reprint, New Delhi, 2004), p. 7, who states that coins had come into circulation in India, 'at least a century before Lydia and China thought of them'; S R Goyal, *The Coinage of Ancient India*, (Jodhpur, 1995), pp. 74-75; etc.

2 M K Dhavalikar, The Beginning of Coinage in India, *World Archaeology* 6(3), (London, 1975), pp. 330-338.

3 Joe Cribb, Investigating the Introduction of Coinage in India—A Review of Recent Research, *Journal of the Numismatic Society of India* 45, (1983), pp. 80-101; Joe Cribb, *The Indian Coinage Tradition: Origins, Continuity and Change*, (Nashik, 2005).

4 A D H Bivar, A Hoard of Ingot Currency of the Median Period from Nush-i-Jan near Malayir, *Iran* 9, (London, 1971), pp. 97-111.

5 M K Dhavalikar, The Beginning of Coinage in India, *World Archaeology* 6(3), (London, 1975), pp. 330-338.

6 Joe Cribb, *The Indian Coinage Tradition : Origins, Continuity and Change*, (Nashik, 2005), especially pp. 18, 52-55.

regular punch-marked coins may be derived from the cup-shaped coins. The so-called bent bars (coins no. 5-7) and the cup-shaped coins have the same style of punch; have the punches arranged in a similar pattern; have the same curved form of flan; have a denomination system, which includes fractional coins; besides, the lower denomination of the cup-shaped coins are 'exact matches in form' to the bent bars. The bent bars, thus, share the features of cup-shaped coins, but do not show the features found on the early series of regular punch-marked coins (coins no. 8-16) derived from the cup-shaped ones, indicating that the bent bars might be earlier than the cup-shaped coins and served as the prototypes for the latter. Therefore, the bent bar coins and the cup-shaped coins represent the earliest phase of Indian coinage, from which all the features of the regular punch-marked coins of the Ganga region were evolved. The Chaman-i-Hazouri hoard contains Greek coins, mostly datable to the fifth century BC; one Iranian imitation of an Athenian coin dated between 390 BC and 350 BC; and a group of locally made adaptations of Greek coins, 'which seem to provide a missing link between Greek coinage and the bent bars', the smaller denominations of bent bars being indistinguishable from 'the smaller denominations of these local adaptations of Greek coinage'. The Gandhāra coins of the Chaman-i-Hazouri hoard are all short and broad bent bars. On the contrary, except for a few specimens which are broad, most of the Gandhāra coins of the Taxila hoard, which was deposited after 323 BC, are narrower, showing that the Chaman-i-Hazouri hoard is earlier than the Taxila hoard, and that the bent bars developed from the broad to narrower shape during the period separating the deposit of the two hoards. The lower denominations of the 'imitations' of Greek coins, resemble the lower denominations of punch-marked coins of Gandhāra and the Ganga region. But they were meant to be 'imitations' of Greek coins in the hoard, as most of them were struck as units, halves, or quarters of Greek or Iranian coinage standards. The standard of the Iranian *shekel* (around 185 grains) was adopted for the Gandhāra coins and for more than half of the 'imitations' of the Greek coins in the Chaman-i-Hazouri hoard. John Allan had also suggested that the bent bars were struck as double the weight of the silver coins struck by the Achaemenian rulers. The discovery of contemporary forgeries of the local coins of Gandhāra at Kauśāmbī shows that these coins were available as prototypes in the Ganga region. On the basis of the above, Cribb suggests that Indian coinage was evolved from the Graeco-Iranian coins. He feels that it would be easy to explain the sudden use of silver for minting coins in India, if it be accepted that 'the whole concept of the monetary use of silver could have been introduced from outside of the sub-continent', the idea coming from the Achaemenian territory, 'being suggested by the *sigloi*' (which have been regarded by some as Graeco-Persian coins).

Greek and Iranian coins were manufactured by the die-striking process. On the contrary, the bent bars, the cup-shaped coins, and the punch-marked coins were manufactured by the punching method. Regarding the Indian 'imitations' of the Greek coins from the Chaman-i-Hazouri hoard, Cribb himself says that they were mostly made by the same method as the local Gandhāra punch-marked coins.[1] Now, if the Indians had learnt the art of minting coins by first imitating the Graeco-Iranian coins, why did they not

1 Joe Cribb, *The Indian Coinage Tradition : Origins, Continuity and Change*, (Nashik, 2005), p. 54.

adopt the die-striking method used in the manufacture of these Graeco-Iranian coins, and evolved a whole new (punch marking) method for manufacturing the imitations of these coins ? Further, to accept Cribb's theory of Graeco-Iranian origin of Indian coinage, one also has to believe, with him,[1] that coinage in India originated in the early fourth century BC, although most of the scholars favour the sixth century BC as the date for the origin of coinage in India.[2]

It is likely that the Indians had evolved their coinage, independent of any foreign influence, and manufactured their coins—bent bar coins, cup-shaped coins and regular punch-marked coins, by the punching method. When they had occasion to manufacture 'imitations' of Graeco-Iranian coins, they adopted the punching method for that too, instead of using the die-striking method by which the Graeco-Iranian coins were manufactured.[3]

---

1 Joe Cribb, *The Indian Coinage Tradition : Origins, Continuity and Change*, (Nashik, 2005), pp. 58-69.

2 See A K Narain and Lallanji Gopal (ed), *Seminar Papers on the Chronology of the Punch Marked Coins*, Varanasi, 1966.

3 Prashant Srivastava, The Theory of the Graeco-Iranian Origin of Indian Coinage : A Reappraisal, in Sushma Srivastava (ed), *Socio-Economic Implications of Commercial Pursuits in Ancient India*, (Allahabad, 2010), pp. 146-151.

2

Antiquity of coinage in India

Most of the scholars are of the view that in the age of the Harappan culture, 'coinage was yet to be evolved'. But in 1926, a silver vase was unearthed in the DK area of Mohenjodaro, which contained pieces of jewellery and some flat silver objects.[1] These silver pieces were regarded by K N Dikshit as 'precursors of punch marked coins of later times'.[2] D D Kosambi also regarded the weights of three of the silver pieces as corresponding to the mean of the class D weight from Mohenjodaro and Harappa, and representing 'the beginning of a coinage system'.[3] This, however, has not

1 See D D Kosambi, On the Origin and Development of Silver Coinage in India, reprinted from *Current Science* 10, (1941), pp. 395-400, in D D Kosambi, *Indian Numismatics*, (New Delhi, 1992), pp. 85-94, on pp. 85-86.

2 K N Dikshit's report on the date of discovery of these pieces, *vide* D D Kosambi, On the Origin and Development of Silver Coinage in India, reprinted from *Current Science* 10, (1941), pp. 395-400, in D D Kosambi, *Indian Numismatics*, (New Delhi, 1992), pp. 85-94, on p. 86.

3 D D Kosambi, On the Origin and Development of Silver Coinage in India, reprinted from *Current Science* 10, (1941), pp. 395-400, in D

been accepted by a vast majority of scholars, writing on the subject.[1]

A passage in the *Ṛigveda* refers to Rudra as wearing a *nishka*, which is *viśvarūpa* in form.[2] This *viśvarūpa* form is understood to mean that probably the *nishka* had numerous symbols marked upon it.[3] It has been suggested that, in this context, *nishka* was a gold coin bearing symbols, and was occasionally used as an ornament, either singly or several of them strewn together in a necklace.[4] It may, however, be mentioned that scholars have pointed out that *viśvarūpa* is also used, in various contexts, for a chariot, cattle, plant, etc.[5] In another passage of the same text, there is an account of the sage, Kakshīvat by name, receiving ten horses and ten *nishkas* from King Bhavya.[6] The *Atharvaveda* refers to the gift of 300 horses, 10,000 cows, 10 necklaces, and 100 *nishkas*.[7] It has been noted in this connection that a gift of ten, or a hundred ornaments (if *nishkas* are taken to mean

---

D Kosambi, *Indian Numismatics*, (New Delhi, 1992), pp. 85-94, on pp. 90-91.

1 For example, A S Altekar, Origin and Early History of Coinage in Ancient India, *Journal of the Numismatic Society of India* 15(1), (1953), pp. 1-26, on pp. 14-15.

2 *Ṛigveda* II. 33. 10.

3 D R Bhandarkar, *Carmichael Lectures on Ancient Indian Numismatics*, (reprint, Patna, 1984), pp. 66-69; A S Altekar, Origin and Early History of Coinage in Ancient India, *Journal of the Numismatic Society of India* 15(1), (1953), pp. 1-26, on p. 11.

4 D R Bhandarkar, *Carmichael Lectures on Ancient Indian Numismatics*, (reprint, Patna, 1984), pp. 66-69.

5 V S Pathak, Semantic Study of Numismatic Terms, *Journal of the Numismatic Society of India* 43, (1981), pp. 1-18, on p. 8.

6 *Ṛigveda* I. 126. 2.

7 *Atharvaveda* XX. 127. 3.

necklaces) would be rather curious. For no one person, or even the members of his family, would need so many pieces of the same ornament to be worn on the body.[1] It would be reasonable to infer that *nishka* was an article of a definite weight and value, if not of a definite size and shape.[2] If it had symbols or devices on it, it could well be a coin-token, if not a coin. Any reference to the use of *nishka* in commercial transactions in the *Ṛigveda* would have provided conclusive evidence to this fact. But we have no such reference in the said text,[3] and cow is the standard medium of exchange.[4] Also, nowhere in the *Ṛigveda* is there any reference to the issue of *nishkas* under any recognized authority. Therefore, it seems more reasonable to infer that, primarily, *nishka* was an ornament of a specific weight,[5] which gradually gave place to a coin denomination of that weight.[6] Manu,[7]

---

1 A S Altekar, Origin and Early History of Coinage in Ancient India, *Journal of the Numismatic Society of India* 15(1), (1953), pp. 1-26, on p. 11.

2 A S Altekar, Origin and Early History of Coinage in Ancient India, *Journal of the Numismatic Society of India* 15(1), (1953), pp. 1-26, on pp. 12-13.

3 A S Altekar, Origin and Early History of Coinage in Ancient India, *Journal of the Numismatic Society of India* 15(1), (1953), pp. 1-26, on pp. 12-13.

4 A S Altekar, Origin and Early History of Coinage in Ancient India, *Journal of the Numismatic Society of India* 15(1), (1953), pp. 1-26, on p. 9.

5 V S Pathak, Semantic Study of Numismatic Terms, *Journal of the Numismatic Society of India* 43, (1981), pp. 1-18, on p. 8.

6 See S R Goyal, *The Coinage of Ancient India*, (Jodhpur, 1995), pp. 55-56.

7 *Manusmṛiti* VIII. 135.

Yājñavalkya,[1] and Vishṇu[2] give the weight of a *nishka* as 320 *rattīs*.

Incidentally, a passage in the *Ṛigveda* depicts Indra as being requested to bestow upon a worshipper, *manās* of gold.[3] The term *mina* denoted a silver or gold ingot of a fixed weight in Babylonia.[4] Could the *manā* of the *Ṛigveda* be the Sanskrit pronunciation of the Babylonian *mina*, and denote a gold coin ? But even if the vedic Indians knew of the *mina*, later total disappearance of the term *manā* from Indian language and literature would tend to show that *manā* 'as a regular weight or coin was foreign to Vedic India'.[5]

Explicit information about the coinage of the period is wanting in the later saṁhitās, brāhmaṇas, and the upanishads. The *Pañchaviṁśabrāhmaṇa* refers to a silver *nishka* as an ornament of the vrātyas.[6] *Nishka* is also mentioned in the *Gopathabrāhmaṇa* in connection with the challenge of Uddālaka Āruṇi, who travelled with a *nishka* attached to his banner, declaring that it would be given to the person who would defeat him in debate.[7] A king is seen in the *Chhāndogyopanishad*, offering his daughter, 1,000 cows, a

---

1 *vide* D R Bhandarkar, *Carmichael Lectures on Ancient Indian Numismatics*, (reprint, Patna, 1984), p. 212.

2 *Vishṇusmṛiti* IV. 10.

3 *Ṛigveda* VIII. 78. 2.

4 A S Altekar, Origin and Early History of Coinage in Ancient India, *Journal of the Numismatic Society of India* 15(1), (1953), pp. 1-26, on p. 14.

5 A S Altekar, Origin and Early History of Coinage in Ancient India, *Journal of the Numismatic Society of India* 15(1), (1953), pp. 1-26, on p. 14.

6 *Pañchaviṁśabrāhmaṇa* XVII. 1-4.

7 *Gopathabrāhmaṇa* I. 3. 16; *cf Śatapathabrāhmaṇa* IX. 4. 1. 1.

horse, a chariot, a village, and a single *nishka*, to a sage to learn from him an esoteric doctrine.[1]

In vedic literature, *nishka* is always mentioned in connection with charity or as a prize.[2] It is to be noted that the typical ornaments, like *khādi* and *rukma*, are never mentioned in the context of charity.[3] This would show that *nishka* in that period was not just an ordinary ornament. It was a piece of well defined weight and had some purchasing value, but not probably a regular coin,[4] as its multiples and submultiples do not find mention in the vedic literature, as also the authority responsible for its issue.

Another gold piece, round in shape, was the *śatamāna* mentioned in later vedic literature. There is a reference to two *śatamānas* attached to the wheel of the royal chariot being offered as *dakshiṇā* to the officiating priest at the time of the *rājasūya yajña*.[5] The *suvarṇa* was, in later times, a gold coin of 80 *rattīs*. It is difficult to say if it was a coin or a piece of gold weighing 80 *rattīs* in the period of the brāhmaṇas as well.[6] In the *Bṛihadāraṇyakopanishad*, it is told that at

1 *Chhāndogyopanishad* IV. 7ff.

2 A S Altekar, Origin and Early History of Coinage in Ancient India, *Journal of the Numismatic Society of India* 15(1), (1953), pp. 1-26, on p. 13.

3 A S Altekar, Origin and Early History of Coinage in Ancient India, *Journal of the Numismatic Society of India* 15(1), (1953), pp. 1-26, on p. 11.

4 A S Altekar, Origin and Early History of Coinage in Ancient India, *Journal of the Numismatic Society of India* 15(1), (1953), pp. 1-26, on pp. 12-13; also S R Goyal, *The Coinage of Ancient India*, (Jodhpur, 1995), p. 55.

5 *Śatapathabrāhmaṇa* V. 4. 32. 4, 26.

6 A S Altekar, Origin and Early History of Coinage in Ancient India, *Journal of the Numismatic Society of India* 15(1), (1953), pp. 1-26,

the time of the *bahudakshiṇā yajña*, Janaka organized a philosophical debate. It was declared that the winner was to receive a thousand cows, with 10 *pādas* attached to the horns of each cow.[1] This *pāda* could be a coin or a metallic (gold ?) piece equal to a quarter of some standard coin—a *nishka*, a *śatamāna*, or a *suvarṇa*.[2] In the *Taittirīyabrāhmaṇa*, there is an account of each chariot racer receiving one *kṛishṇala*.[3]

In later vedic literature, *nishka*, *śatamāna*, *suvarṇa*, and *pāda* are mentioned, always in connection with the fee paid to the priests on auspicious occasions, and never as ornaments. It is not mentioned whether or not they bore any mark or device on their surface. It has been suggested that they might have been used as currency,[4] but as things were very cheap, occasions when transactions were made with the help of gold currency would have been very rare indeed, and usually barter was in vogue. Silver and copper currency, which would have been required for smaller transactions, are nowhere mentioned in the literature of the period.[5]

While earlier literature referred to gold pieces only in the context of generous gifts, the literature of the period from about the sixth century BC refers to coins in

---

on p. 16.

1 *Bṛihadāraṇyakopanishad* III. 1. 1-2.

2 A S Altekar, Origin and Early History of Coinage in Ancient India, *Journal of the Numismatic Society of India* 15(1), (1953), pp. 1-26, on p. 17.

3 *Taittirīyabrāhmaṇa* I. 3. 6. 7.

4 A S Altekar, Origin and Early History of Coinage in Ancient India, *Journal of the Numismatic Society of India* 15(1), (1953), pp. 1-26, on pp. 17-18.

5 A S Altekar, Origin and Early History of Coinage in Ancient India, *Journal of the Numismatic Society of India* 15(1), (1953), pp. 1-26, on pp. 18-19.

connection with ordinary commercial transactions. Thus, in the *Ashṭādhyāyī*, articles worth one, two, and three *nishka*(*s*) are called *naishkikaṁ*, *dvi-naishkikaṁ*, and *tri-naishkikaṁ*, respectively,[1] while terms like *naishka-śatika* and *naishka-sāhassrika* denoted persons worth a hundred and a thousand *nishkas*, respectively.[2] The term *nishka* also occurs in the Jātaka literature. Thus, in the *Kuhakajātaka*, a person misappropriates a deposit of a hundred *nishkas* placed with him.[3] *Pāda*- or quarter-*nishka* is referred to by Patañjali.[4] In the *Bhūridattajātaka*, the *bodhisattva*, a nāga, earns for a snake charmer, a hundred thousand coins (*suvarṇas*) a day.[5] The *Udayajātaka* refers to gold *māshakas*.[6] Whether these *māshakas* were gold coins weighing about 1/16 of a *suvarṇa*, or 'small medallic pieces' of the same weight used for preparing necklaces,[7] is not certain. *Śatamāna* as a gold

---

1 *Ashṭādhyāyī* V. 1. 30.

2 *Ashṭādhyāyī* V. 2. 119.

3 Jātaka no. 89. See E B Cowell (ed), *The Jātaka or Stories of the Buddha's Former Births*, translated from the Pāli by various hands 1, (reprint, Delhi, 2005), pp. 218-219.

4 *vide* A S Altekar, Origin and Early History of Coinage in Ancient India, *Journal of the Numismatic Society of India* 15(1), (1953), pp. 1-26, on p. 20.

5 Jātaka no. 543. See E B Cowell (ed), *The Jātaka or Stories of the Buddha's Former Births*, translated from the Pāli by various hands 6, (reprint, Delhi, 2005), pp. 80-113, on pp. 98, 101.

6 Jātaka no. 458. See E B Cowell (ed), *The Jātaka or Stories of the Buddha's Former Births*, translated from the Pāli by various hands 4, (reprint, Delhi, 2005), pp. 66-70, on p. 68.

7 A S Altekar, Origin and Early History of Coinage in Ancient India, *Journal of the Numismatic Society of India* 15(1), (1953), pp. 1-26, on p. 20.

coin is mentioned by both Pāṇini and Kātyāyana.[1] Pāṇini explains *śātamāna* as an object purchased for a *śatamāna*.[2] Some scholars opine that *śatamāna* literally means a *māna* (standard) of hundred, and might have weighed a hundred *rattīs*.[3] But, in view of the fact that both Manu[4] and Yājñavalkya[5] refer to *śatamāna* as of 320 *rattīs*,[6] some scholars suggest that *mañjāḍī*, weighing about 3.2 *rattīs*, was the *māna*.[7]

There is evidence from the *Maitrāyaṇīsaṁhitā* of the *Yajurveda*,[8] the *Śatapathabrāhmaṇa*,[9] and the *Kātyāyanaśrautasūtra*,[10] to show that silver *śatamāna* existed side by side with a gold one. V S Agrawala identifies the silver bent bar coins, weighing about 175 grains (= 100

---

1 A S Altekar, Origin and Early History of Coinage in Ancient India, *Journal of the Numismatic Society of India* 15(1), (1953), pp. 1-26, on p. 20.

2 *Ashṭādhyāyī* V. 1. 27.

3 A B Keith, The Period of the Later Saṁhitās, the Brāhmaṇas, the Āraṇyakas, and the Upanishads, Chapter V, in E J Rapson (ed), *The Cambridge History of India* 1, (reprint, Delhi, 1987), pp. 102-133, on p. 122; A S Altekar, Origin and Early History of Coinage in Ancient India, *Journal of the Numismatic Society of India* 15(1), (1953), pp. 1-26, on p. 20; S K Maity, *Early India Coins and Currency System*, (New Delhi, 1970), p. 21.

4 *Manusmṛiti* VIII. 135-137.

5 *Yājñavalkyasmṛiti* I. 364-365.

6 See D C Sircar, *Studies in Indian Coins*, (Delhi, 1968), p. 51.

7 S K Chakrabortty, *A Study of Ancient Indian Numismatics*, (Mymensingh, 1931), p. 27; *cf* D C Sircar, *Studies in Indian Coins*, (Delhi, 1968), pp. 59-60.

8 *Maitrāyaṇīsaṁhitā* II. 2. 2.

9 *Śatapathabrāhmaṇa* XIII. 42. 10.

10 *Kātyāyanaśrautasūtra* XVI. 45.

rattīs), as silver *śatamāna*.[1] But scholars have pointed out that *śatamāna* in the *Śatapathabrāhmaṇa* (as also in Sāyaṇa's commentary) is referred to as round in shape, and not as long which is the case with the bent bar pieces.[2] A S Altekar likens some Kosala coins weighing between 75 and 79 grains with *arddha-śatamāna*, the coins from the Paila hoard weighing 44 grains with *pāda-śatamāna*, and the Sonepur silver punch-marked coins weighing 21 grains with *pādārddha-śatamāna* or *śāṇa*.[3] According to the *Mahābhārata*, eight *śāṇas* constitute a *śatamāna*.[4] Later on, however, this silver *śatamāna* and its submultiples were replaced by the silver *kārshāpaṇa* currency.[5]

Kārshāpaṇa and its submultiples are mentioned quite frequently in the *Ashṭādhyāyī* and the *Tripiṭaka*. The former text refers to *kārshāpaṇa*,[6] *arddha-kārshāpaṇa*,[7] *pāda-kārshāpaṇa*,[8] *dvi-māshaka* (one-eighth *kārshāpaṇa*), and

---

1 V S Agrawala, Ancient Coins as known to Pāṇini, *Journal of the Numismatic Society of India* 15(1), (1953), pp. 27-41, on p. 30. See also S K Maity, *Early India Coins and Currency System*, (New Delhi, 1970), p. 24.

2 See S R Goyal, *The Coinage of Ancient India*, (Jodhpur, 1995), pp. 60-61.

3 A S Altekar, Origin and Early History of Coinage in Ancient India, *Journal of the Numismatic Society of India* 15(1), (1953), pp. 1-26, on p. 21.

4 *Mahābhārata* III. 134. 14.

5 A S Altekar, Origin and Early History of Coinage in Ancient India, *Journal of the Numismatic Society of India* 15(1), (1953), pp. 1-26, on p. 22.

6 *Ashṭādhyāyī* V. 1. 29.

7 *Ashṭādhyāyī* V. 1. 49.

8 *Ashṭādhyāyī* V. 1. 34.

māsha (one-sixteenth *kārshāpaṇa*).[1] The coin is referred to as *kahāpaṇa* in the *Vinayapiṭaka*,[2] the *Majjhimanikāya*,[3] and the *Aṅguttaranikāya*.[4] While the *Vinayapiṭaka* also refers to *pāda-kahāpaṇa*,[5] Jātaka tales refer to *arddha-kārshāpaṇa*, *pāda-kārshāpaṇa*, *chatur-māshaka*, *tri-māshaka*, *dvi-māshaka*, *eka-māshaka*, and *arddha-māshaka*.[6] Most of these coin denominations have been identified with the actual specimens found. Thus, silver currency was quite well-established at the time of Pāṇini, the *Tripiṭaka*, and the Jātaka literature.

The dates of Pāṇini, the Jātaka literature, and the śrautasūtras are controversial. Some scholars place Pāṇini as early as the seventh century BC,[7] although the generally accepted date for him is the fifth century BC.[8] The generally

1 A S Altekar, Origin and Early History of Coinage in Ancient India, *Journal of the Numismatic Society of India* 15(1), (1953), pp. 1-26, on p. 22.

2 *Vinayapiṭaka*, edited by H Oldenberg, 5 vols, (Pāli Text Society, London, 1873-1883), VIII. 1. 1.

3 *Majjhimanikāya*, edited by V Treckner and R Chalmers, 3 vols, (Pāli Text Society, London, 1888-1904), III, p. 168.

4 *Aṅguttaranikāya*, edited by R Morris and E Hardy, 5 vols, (Pāli Text Society, London, 1885-1890), V, p. 83.

5 *Vinayapiṭaka*, edited by H Oldenberg, 5 vols, (Pāli Text Society, London, 1873-1883), III, p. 49.

6 *vide* A S Altekar, Origin and Early History of Coinage in Ancient India, *Journal of the Numismatic Society of India* 15(1), (1953), pp. 1-26, on p. 23, and n. 2.

7 See V S Agrawala, *India as known to Pāṇini*, (Lucknow, 1953), pp. 455ff.

8 V S Agrawala, *India as known to Pāṇini*, (Lucknow, 1953), p. 475; also M A Mahendale, Language and Literature, Chapter XVIA, in R C Majumdar, A D Pusalker, and A K Majumdar (ed), *The Age of*

favoured date for the *Tripiṭaka* is *c* 450 BC,[1] while the śrautasūtras may be placed about a century earlier.[2] There are references to a well established system of currency in these texts dating between *c* 600 BC and *c* 450 BC. However, some recent writers on the subject, accepting the view that the *nirvāṇa* of the Buddha should be dated *c* 400 BC or even later,[3] suggest that India's first coins were issued as late as the beginning of the fourth century BC,[4] or even *c* 350 BC.[5] Bhandarkar's view that coinage was in vogue amidst the vedic Aryans as early as the middle of the third millennium BC,[6] is regarded as untenable by a vast majority of scholars. Even Cunningham's view, that the antiquity of

---

Imperial Unity, (The History and Culture of the Indian People 2), (Bombay, 1980), pp. 243-287, on pp. 268-269.

1 A S Altekar, Origin and Early History of Coinage in Ancient India, *Journal of the Numismatic Society of India* 15(1), (1953), pp. 1-26, on p. 24.

2 A S Altekar, Origin and Early History of Coinage in Ancient India, *Journal of the Numismatic Society of India* 15(1), (1953), pp. 1-26, on p. 24.

3 See Heinz Bechert, *Die Datierung des Historischen Buddha*, 2 vols, (Göttingen, 1991-1992), translated from the German as *When did Buddha Live—The Controversy of the Dating of the Historical Buddha*, (Delhi, 1995).

4 See Joe Cribb, Dating India's Earliest Coins, in M Taddei and J Schotsman (ed), *South Asian Archaeology 1983*, (Naples, 1985), pp. 535-554. Also Joe Cribb, *The Indian Coinage Tradition—Origins, Continuity and Change*, (Nashik, 2005), Appendix 2.

5 Joe Cribb, Punch-marked Coins—Approaches to New Research, *Oriental Numismatic Society Newsletter* 146, (Autumn 1995), pp. 7-8.

6 D R Bhandarkar, *Carmichael Lectures on Ancient Indian Numismatics*, (reprint Patna, 1984), p. 71.

coinage in India may be taken as far back as 1000 BC, is not substantiated by literary or archaeological evidence.

The theory of placing the beginning of coinage in India in the sixth century BC seems to be supported by archaeological evidence as well. No punch-marked coins are available from strata lower than those of the Northern Black Polished Ware.[1] Even with the Northern Black Polished Ware (sixth century BC to first century BC), the punch-marked coins at sites, like Atranjikhera, Kauśāmbī, Rajghat, Rupar, Hastinapur, etc, are found in strata later than the earliest phase of the Northern Black Polished Ware.[2] It is felt by some scholars that the economy of the post-Harappan chalcolithic and other cultures (like the Painted Grey Ware culture) was not so developed as to need or support a coinage in gold. From about the sixth century BC, which is marked by the widespread use of iron, the use of Northern Black Polished Ware, and the beginning of the second urbanization, the atmosphere for the introduction of coinage was there, and silver and copper punch-marked coins were issued.

Silver was scarce in India, while silver punch-marked coins are abundant. Silver could have been brought from Afghanistan, or Iran, or even Babylonia, as a result of trade. This metal is not referred to in the *Ṛigveda*, and only rarely in early vedic literature[3], showing that it was not much in use in that period. Though some scholars have tried to show that silver was not scarce in India, it could hardly have been enough to meet the need of issuing huge quantities of punch-

---

1 S R Goyal, *The Coinage of Ancient India*, (Jodhpur, 1995), p. 67.

2 S R Goyal, *The Coinage of Ancient India*, (Jodhpur, 1995), p. 68.

3 S R Goyal, *The Coinage of Ancient India*, (Jodhpur, 1995), p. 55.

marked coins, and had to be imported from elsewhere.[1] In fact, the *Periplus*,[2] and also a few other Greek works,[3] mention the import of silver in India. There is also a suggestion that the term *kārshāpaṇa* is of Iranian origin.[4] It is quite likely that silver was imported into India from Iran at the time of the rise of Achaemenian imperialism and the beginning of the rise of Magadhan imperialism in the sixth century BC.[5] Some scholars have expressed doubts regarding the presence of coinage before 700 BC anywhere in the world.[6]

---

1 See S R Goyal, *The Coinage of Ancient India*, (Jodhpur, 1995), pp. 69-70.

2 *Periplus Maris Erythraei*, translated from the Greek and annotated by W H Schoff, as *The Periplus of the Erythraean Sea*, (reprint, New Delhi, 2001), pp. 24, 25, 26, 31, 33, 42.

3 See S R Goyal, *The Coinage of Ancient India*, (Jodhpur, 1995), p. 70.

4 A K Narain, A Note on *Kārshāpaṇa*, *Journal of the Numismatic Society of India* 19(2), (1957), pp. 181-183; see also Prashant Srivastava, *Encyclopaedia of India Coins (Ancient Coins of Northern India, up to* circa *650 AD)* 1, (Delhi, 2012), pp. 198-200.

5 See S R Goyal, *The Coinage of Ancient India*, (Jodhpur, 1995), p. 70.

6 See S R Goyal, *The Coinage of Ancient India*, (Jodhpur, 1995), p. 54.

3

Introduction of the die-striking mode of fabrication of coins in India

There is some controversy among scholars regarding the origins of the technique of die-striking in India. Prinsep is of the view that the Indian system of die-striking was, actually, of foreign origin.[1] But a comparison between the punch-marked coins and die-struck coins reveals that while the symbols on punch-marked coins were impressed by separate punches, perhaps even at different times,[2] the device on die-struck coins was actually a group of symbols and/or legend, impressed by a single punch (called *die*). As such, it has often been said that the die-striking process was 'the logical development of the technique of minting coins by punching

1 *vide* S K Chakrabortty, *A Study of Ancient Indian Numismatics*, (Mymensingh, 1931), p. 123.

2 *Contra* E H C Walsh, Indian Punch-marked Coins, *Journal of the Royal Asiatic Society of Great Britain and Ireland*, Centenary Supplement, p. 187, *vide* S K Chakrabortty, *A Study of Ancient Indian Numismatics*, (Mymensingh, 1931), p. 108, who says that 'all the obverse marks were punched on the metal when heated, and so, probably, at one time'.

one side of the blank with several dies'. It is believed that the process of evolution of die-striking method from the punch-marking method involved four stages.[1] In the first stage, a group of symbols, forming a distinct type, was impressed by a single die which did not cover the whole flan of the piece, and the reverse remained blank. In the second stage, a die was engraved or embedded on the anvil so that the reverse of the blank also received a device and/or legend. In the third stage, the obverse die covered the whole face of the blank, but the reverse die remained smaller than the blank. The fourth and final stage is marked by the double-die-struck coins, where both the obverse and the reverse dies cover the whole face of the blank.

V A Smith opined, "The final adoption of the 'double-die' system was undoubtedly due to Greek and Roman example".[2] This statement of Smith comes in for strong criticism at the hands of D R Bhandarkar, who says, 'What Smith's remark comes to is that the Indians were, of course, capable of introducing improvement into and thus developing the technique of manufacture of coins before the advent of the Greeks, but their last step, although it was the natural culmination of their gradual advance in the indigenous numismatic art, they could affect only when the Macedonians came to teach them!!!'[3] Bhandarkar finds support from the statement of E Thomas that Indians had

1 Edward Thomas, *Ancient Indian Weights*, (Marsden's Numismata Orientalia 1, London, 1874), p. 55; D R Bhandarkar, *Carmichael Lectures on Ancient Indian Numismatics*, (reprint Patna, 1984), p. 151.

2 V A Smith, *Imperial Gazetteer of India* 2, p. 137.

3 D R Bhandarkar, *Carmichael Lectures on Ancient Indian Numismatics*, (reprint, Patna, 1984), pp. 151-152.

made all the advances from the punch-marking to the die-striking system, before the advent of the Greeks in India.[1]

Advocates of both the theories, regarding the origins of the technique of manufacturing die-struck coins, may be partially correct. Once the technique of die-striking was learnt in one region of the Indian subcontinent, it might have taken a long time to spread over the different regions of this vast land.[2] Then, there might also have been the inherent reluctance in adopting a later but better method as long as possible.[3]

Let us take into consideration certain points :

1. Athenian 'owls' are believed to have been in circulation in Afghanistan and, perhaps, even the frontier regions of northwestern India, and imitations of these 'owls' were manufactured in these regions,[4] during the Achaemenian period.[5]
2. S K Chakrabortty believes that the *Rākshasa* type die-struck coins from Takshaśilā, bearing on the obverse the head of a *rākshasa* with short ears and protruded tongue,[6] resembling the Gorgon's

1 Edward Thomas, *Ancient Indian Weights*, (Marsden's Numismata Orientalia 1, London, 1874), p. 55; D R Bhandarkar, *Carmichael Lectures on Ancient Indian Numismatics*, (reprint Patna, 1984), p. 55.

2 *Cf* S K Chakrabortty, *A Study of Ancient Indian Numismatics*, (Mymensingh, 1931), pp. 122-123.

3 S K Chakrabortty, *A Study of Ancient Indian Numismatics*, (Mymensingh, 1931), pp. 121-122.

4 D R Bhandarkar, *Carmichael Lectures on Ancient Indian Numismatics*, (reprint, Patna, 1984), p. 29.

5 A K Narain, *The Indo-Greeks*, (Oxford, 1957), p. 4.

6 Alexander Cunningham, *Coins of Ancient India*, (reprint Varanasi, 1971), pl. III. 7.

head, were struck in imitation of the Greek coins of Eretria,[1] issued prior to the Persian Wars of 490 BC to 480 BC.[2] Chakrabortty places these imitation coins of the *Rākshasa* type in the fifth century BC.[3]

3. Some locally produced 'Kabul' coins from the Chaman-i-Hazouri hoard, which are taken to 'represent the earliest stage in the development of the indigenous Indian coinage',[4] bear on the obverse the device of two heads of bulls, face to face.[5] This device is taken to have been copied from some Greek prototype, and the coins are believed to 'remind us of the early electrums of Lydia'.[6]
4. Achaemenian coins have been found in a hoard discovered at Chaman-i-Hazouri in the Kabul area.[7]
5. Sophytes, an eastern *satrap* of the Achaemenians, 'a Greek with the semblance of an Iranian name',[8] issued die-struck pieces in northwestern India,

---

1 Barclay V Head, *Coins of the Ancients*, pl. V. 25.

2 S K Chakrabortty, *A Study of Ancient Indian Numismatics*, (Mymensingh, 1931), p. 213.

3 S K Chakrabortty, *A Study of Ancient Indian Numismatics*, (Mymensingh, 1931), p. 126.

4 Wilfried Pieper, in Osmund Bopearachchi and Wilfried Pieper, *Ancient Indian Coins*, (Brepols, Turnhout, 1998), p. 9.

5 Osmund Bepearachchi and Aman ur Rahman, *Pre-Kushana Coins in Pakistan*, (Karachi, 1995), Catalogue, coin no. 1.

6 Osmund Bepearachchi and Aman ur Rahman, *Pre-Kushana Coins in Pakistan*, (Karachi, 1995), p. 55.

7 See B N Mukherjee and P K D Lee, *The Technology of Indian Coinage*, (Calcutta, 1988), p. 67.

8 A K Narain, *The Indo-Greeks*, (Oxford, 1957), p. 5.

bearing the Greek symbol, *caduceus*,[1] during the decline of the Achaemenian power in Iran.[2]

6. Indian die-struck coins appear for the first time, perhaps, at Takshaśilā in northwestern India.[3] Single-die-struck coins from Takshaśilā have been dated to the end of the fourth century BC, or even earlier by some scholars,[4] although the evidence of the Bhir mound hoard from Takshaśilā, dated to the last quarter of the fourth century BC by Marshall,[5] and containing an Achaemenian *siglos*, two *tetradrachms* of Alexander of Macedon, one *tetradrachm* of Philip III Arrhidios, 33 silver bent bar (wheel-marked) coins, 79 pieces bearing a single punch each, and 1055 regular silver punch-marked coins, (die-struck coins being conspicuous by their absence),[6] would show that at this time, punch-marked coins 'formed the bulk of the local currency' at Takshaśilā.
7. It has been said that the single-die-struck pieces from Takshaśilā bear 'the impress of the die (which)

---

1 Percy Gardner, *The Catalogue of the Coins of the Greek and Scythic Kings of Bactria and India, in the British Museum, London*, (reprint, New Delhi, 1971), pl. I. 1.

2 A K Narain, *The Indo-Greeks*, (Oxford, 1957), p. 4.

3 *Cf* E J Rapson, *Indian Coins*, (Strassburg, 1897), p. 14.

4 See A N Lahiri, Archaic Coins from Northern India, *Journal of the Numismatic Society of India* 35, (1973), pp. 1-38, on p. 32. *Contra* John H Marshall, *Taxila* 2, (reprint, Delhi, 1975), p. 756, who says that it would be unsafe to place the local coins of Takshaśilā before the third century BC.

5 John H Marshall, *Taxila* 1, (reprint, Delhi, 1975), p. 106; *ibid.* 2, p. 843.

6 John H Marshall, *Taxila* 1, (reprint, Delhi, 1975), pp. 105-106; *ibid.* 2, pp. 843-844, 845.

was left enclosed in a deep incuse square', which shows that the method of striking was 'peculiarly Indian'.[1] But the square incuse is seen, not only on the reverse of the Athenian 'owls'[2] datable to the mid-fifth century BC,[3] but an oblong incuse is also seen on the reverse of the Achaemenian *darics*.[4] The coin of Sophytes also seems to bear a reverse incuse.[5] This would also render the argument that because the single-die-struck coins from Sultanpur, near Wai in Satara district, bear an incuse impression,[6] they should be dated quite early and be regarded as 'the earliest examples of the die-struck coins of India',[7] less forceful.

It has been seen in Chapter 1 that, when people of northwestern India and its borderlands had occasion to 'imitate' die-struck Greek coins, they manufactured these 'imitations' by the punching method, as is clear from such

---

1 E J Rapson, *Indian Coins*, (Strassburg, 1897), p. 14.

2 Percy Gardner, *A History of Ancient Coinage (700-300 BC)*, (Oxford, 1918), pl. II. 9.12.

3 See Ewald Junge, *World Coin Encyclopedia*, (Barrie & Jenkins, London, 1984), p. 29.

4 Percy Gardner, *A History of Ancient Coinage (700-300 BC)*, (Oxford, 1918), pl. I. 7.

5 Percy Gardner, *The Catalogue of the Coins of the Greek and Scythic Kings of Bactria and India, in the British Museum, London*, (reprint, New Delhi, 1971), pl. I. 1.

6 John Allan, *The Catalogue of the Coins of Ancient India, in the British Museum, London*, (London, 1936), pl. I. 16-19.

7 See Bela Lahiri, Foreign Elements in Local and Tribal Coins, in A M Shastri (ed), *Foreign Elements in Indian Indigenous Coins*, (Memoirs of the Numismatic Society of India 8), (Varanasi, 1982), pp. 136-143, on p. 137.

'imitations' in the Chaman-i-Hazouri hoard, and not by the die-striking method. However, it would appear that the people of northwestern India and its borderlands, who were familiar with the die-struck Greek and Achaemenian coins, and who, along with the people of Afghanistan, were striking imitations of the Athenian 'owls', Gorgon's head type of Eretria (*c* fifth century BC), and the two bulls' heads face to face type of Lydia, might have felt the impact of the technique of die-striking of the foreigners. The presence of the square incuse would seem to support, rather than discredit, this conjecture. But the very fact that various stages in the evolution of the die-striking process are evident in India, even at Takshaśilā, would show that the Indians had started making independent attempts to impress a collection of symbols and/or legend from a single punch (or die) instead of using a separate punch for each symbol. Those regions, which came into contact with the more advanced technique of the Greeks and the Achaemenians, might have skipped over some intermediate stages, while those regions which were left to themselves, had to pass through the different stages of evolution of the die-striking system.[1] Some of the latter regions even might have skipped over some of the stages due to the gradual spread of the technique from northwestern India into the *madhyadeśa*. Perhaps, this would explain the fact that all the regions of India do not provide evidence of going through all the stages in the evolution of the die-striking process.[2]

---

1 *Cf* S K Chakrabortty, *A Study of Ancient Indian Numismatics*, (Mymensingh, 1931), p. 122.

2 Prashant Srivastava, Die-striking Mode of Fabrication of Coins : Its Origin in India, *Journal of the Numismatic Society of India* 70, (2008), pp. 28-31.

4

Introduction of legends on coins

The earliest available coins of India, that is the punch-marked coins, are uninscribed. Indians started inscribing their coins later on. There is some controversy among scholars regarding the origin of the Indian practice of engraving legends on coins. While one group of scholars feels that there was some foreign inspiration behind the beginning of this tradition, another group regards it as of indigenous origin.

The first invasion of India in recorded history was that of the Persians, during the Achaemenian period. But, as early Persians coins are anepigraphous,[1] they could not have influenced ancient Indian coins in respect of legends. However, the influence of the coins of the Greeks (of Greece Proper and of the Greek colonies in western Asia), Romans, Imperial Parthians (the Arsakids), and other foreign powers, is visible on the legends found on early Indian coins.

There are some scholars, who advocate the theory that the Indians started the practice of inscribing their coins

---

1 *Cf* Charles Seltman, *Greek Coins*, (London, 1955), pp. 62ff.

under Indo-Greek influence.[1] But others reject this theory, and believe that the practice of inscribing coins was an indigenous development in India itself.[2] They hold that the earliest inscribed coins of India come from Eran,[3] and, as, according to them, the coins are datable to the third century BC,[4] they antedate Indo-Greek coins; and, as the city of Eran could not have had any possible contact with Greek coins,[5]

---

1 See S K Chakrabortty, *A Study of Ancient Indian Numismatics*, (Mymensingh, 1931), p. 138; D C Sircar, in D C Sircar (ed), *Early Indian Indigenous Coins*, (Calcutta, 1970), p. 6; Jaiprakash, On Ancient Indian Coin-legends, *Journal of the Numismatic Society of India* 23, (1961), pp. 241-258, on p. 245; M P Joshi, *Morphogensis of the Kuṇindas : A Numismatic Overview*, (Almora, 1989), p. 87, n. 185; S R Goyal, *Indigenous Coins of Early India*, (Jodhpur, 1994), p. 50; etc.

2 *Cf* A N Lahiri, Impact of Foreign Coins on the Legends of Early Indigenous Issues, in A M Shastri (ed), *Foreign Elements in Indian Indigenous Coins*, (Memoirs of the Numismatic Society of India 8), (Varanasi, 1982), pp. 68-79, on p. 69; Bela Lahiri, India's Earliest Inscribed Coins : The City Issues, *Journal of the Numismatic Society of India* 38(2), (1976), pp. 35-54, on p. 35; Bela Lahiri, Foreign Elements in Local and Tribal Coins, in A M Shastri (ed), *Foreign Elements in Indian Indigenous Coins*, (Memoirs of the Numismatic Society of India 8), (Varanasi, 1982), pp. 136-143, on p. 138.

3 A N Lahiri, Impact of Foreign Coins on the Legends of Early Indigenous Issues, in A M Shastri (ed), *Foreign Elements in Indian Indigenous Coins*, (Memoirs of the Numismatic Society of India 8), (Varanasi, 1982), pp. 68-79, on p. 70; Bela Lahiri, *Indigenous States of Northern India*, (Calcutta, 1974), p. 81.

4 John Allan, *Catalogue of the Coins of Ancient India, in the British Museum, London*, (London, 1936), p. 140.

5 A N Lahiri, Impact of Foreign Coins on the Legends of Early Indigenous Issues, in A M Shastri (ed), *Foreign Elements in Indian Indigenous Coins*, (Memoirs of the Numismatic Society of India 8), (Varanasi, 1982), pp. 68-79, on p. 71.

Indians must have started inscribing their coins on their own. It has also been pointed out that one of the coins from Eran[1] bears the legend, *Dhamapālasa*, in the negative, because the die-cutter was inexperienced in engraving legends, and 'made the die in the positive so that the letters were impressed on the coin in the negative'.[2] Bela Lahiri feels that had 'the Indians learnt the method of inscribing coins from the monetary issues of the foreigners they would not have made this initial mistake which was corrected afterwards'.[3]

Possibly, Indians did not learn the art of inscribing coins from the Indo-Greeks. The Takshaśilā coins, bearing the legend, *Hirañasame*,[4] served as the prototype[5] for the *Hirañasame* coins of the Indo-Greek ruler, Agathokles,[6] and have rightly been dated earlier than the Indo-Greek coins. It has been observed that the *Hirañasame* coins, as well as several other coins from Takshaśilā, bear an incuse impression. A similar incuse impression is also to be seen

---

1 John Allan, *Catalogue of the Coins of Ancient India, in the British Museum, London*, (London, 1936), pl. XVIII. 6.

2 Bela Lahiri, Foreign Elements in Local and Tribal Coins, in A M Shastri (ed), *Foreign Elements in Indian Indigenous Coins*, (Memoirs of the Numismatic Society of India 8), (Varanasi, 1982), pp. 136-143, on p. 138.

3 Bela Lahiri, Foreign Elements in Local and Tribal Coins, in A M Shastri (ed), *Foreign Elements in Indian Indigenous Coins*, (Memoirs of the Numismatic Society of India 8), (Varanasi, 1982), pp. 136-143, on p. 138.

4 John Allan, *Catalogue of the Coins of Ancient India, in the British Museum, London*, (London, 1936), pl. XXXIV. 7.

5 John Allan, *Catalogue of the Coins of Ancient India, in the British Museum, London*, (London, 1936), p. cxxxii.

6 R B Whitehead, *Catalogue of the Coins in the Punjab Museum, Lahore* 1, The Indo-Greek Coins, (Oxford, 1914), pl. II. 52.

on the coins of only two rulers among the Indo-Greeks, namely Pantaleon and Agathokles. On this basis, it has been concluded that these coins from Takshaśilā are to be placed earlier than Pantaleon and Agathokles.[1] Again, the cast coins, bearing legends, like *Upagodasa*,[2] *Upātikyā*,[3] *Kāḍasa*,[4] etc, have been dated earlier than the Indo-Greek coins by some prominent scholars, like John Allan.[5]

Before rejecting outright the theory of foreign inspiration behind the adoption of the practice of inscribing coins by the India, we must take into consideration certain points :

1. The Greeks were inscribing their coins since quite early times, and there was a continuous flow of these coins into Afghanistan and the borderlands of northwestern India, even during the Achaemenian period, due to trade and commerce.[6]
2. The early Achaemenian *sigloi* were uninscribed, but the later coins of this type bear legend, perhaps on being 'inspired by the Greek numismatic art'.[7]

---

1 See C C Dasgupta, *The Development of the Kharoṣṭhī Script*, (Calcutta, 1958), pp. 23-27, on p. 26.

2 John Allan, *Catalogue of the Coins of Ancient India, in the British Museum, London*, (London, 1936), pl. XXXV. 18.

3 Alexander Cunningham, *Coins of Ancient India*, (reprint, Varanasi, 1971), pl. VIII. 2.

4 John Allan, *Catalogue of the Coins of Ancient India, in the British Museum, London*, (London, 1936), pl. XIX. 14.

5 John Allan, *Catalogue of the Coins of Ancient India, in the British Museum, London*, (London, 1936), pp. xcii, cxlv, cxlvi.

6 *Cf* A K Narain, *The Indo-Greeks*, (Oxford, 1957), p. 4.

7 See Jaiprakash, On Ancient Indian Coin-legends, *Journal of the Numismatic Society of India* 23, (1961), pp. 241-258, on p. 245.

3. The Athenian 'owls', which were in circulation in Afghanistan and the frontier regions of northwestern India,[1] bear the Greek legend, *Athe*, for 'Athens', the name of the city, on the reverse.[2] This had become the fixed type of the city of Athens, latest by the middle of the fifth century BC,[3] if not earlier.
4. Imitations of these 'owls' of Athens were struck locally in Afghanistan and northwestern borderlands of India, during the Achaemenian period.[4]
5. Some of these imitation 'owls' bear the Greek legend, *Aig*, in place of *Athe* of the original Athenian coins.[5] B V Head interprets *Aig* as, perhaps, referring to the Aigloi, a people placed by Herodotos to the north of Bactria.[6] This would, perhaps, show that, in some cases, people in these regions were not only

---

1 D R Bhandarkar, *Carmichael Lectures on Ancient Indian Numismatics*, (reprint, Patna, 1984), p. 29. *Cf* George Macdonald, Ancient Greek (Athenian and Macedonian) Coins in India, Appendix to Chapter XV, in E J Rapson (ed), *The Cambridge History of India* 1, (reprint, Delhi, 1987), pp. 346-350, on p. 346; A K Narain, *The Indo-Greeks*, (Oxford, 1957), p. 4.

2 See Percy Gardner, *History of Ancient Coinage (700 BC-300 BC)*, (Oxford, 1918), pl. II. 12.

3 Ewald Junge, *World Coin Encyclopedia*, (London, 1984), p. 29.

4 See D R Bhandarkar, *Carmichael Lectures on Ancient Indian Numismatics*, (reprint, Patna, 1984), p. 29. *Cf* George Macdonald, Ancient Greek (Athenian and Macedonian) Coins in India, Appendix to Chapter XV, in E J Rapson (ed), *The Cambridge History of India* 1, (reprint, Delhi, 1987), pp. 346-350, on p. 346; A K Narain, *The Indo-Greeks*, (Oxford, 1957), p. 4.

5 E J Rapson (ed), *The Cambridge History of India*, I, (reprint, Delhi, 1987), pl. I. 8.

6 *Cf* George Macdonald, Ancient Greek (Athenian and Macedonian) Coins in India, Appendix to Chapter XV, in E J Rapson (ed), *The*

imitating the 'owls' of Athens, but also introducing their tribal name on coins.[1]

6. In the Punjab region were found certain Attic silver *drachms*, bearing the legend, *Sophytou*, in the Greek script.[2] This Sophytes appears to be a satrap of the eastern province of the Achaemenian empire, and issued coins during the decline of the power of the Achaemenian dynasty.[3]
7. The inscribed coins from Takshaśilā, in northwestern India, were placed by John Allan in the first quarter

---

Cambridge History of India 1, (reprint, Delhi, 1987), pp. 346-350, on p. 347; A K Narain, *The Indo-Greeks*, (Oxford, 1957), p. 4, n. 3.

1 It might be observed that the tribe, normally, would have put the legend in the Greek script, if the head(s) of the tribe were acquainted with the script, and, one can even say, if the people, for whom the coins were issued, were also acquainted with the Greek script, and could understand that the Greek legend stands for the name of their tribe, Aigloi. But them we have evidence of Greek colonies of the Thracians (?) at Nysa, and of the Branchidae in Sogdiana, to the north of Bactria (A K Narain, *The Indo-Greeks*, (Oxford, 1957), p. 3, and ns. 4, 5), and the people of Bactria, and of regions to the north of this province, would have been familiar with the Greek script. *Cf* Schlumberger (*Trésors Monétaires d'Afghanistan*, p. 4, *vide* A K Narain, *The Indo-Greeks*, (Oxford, 1957), p. 4, n. 3), who regards *Aig* as denoting the name of a satrap.

2 Percy Gardner, *Catalogue of the Goins of the Greek and Scythic Kings of Bactria and India, in the British Museum, London*, (reprint, New Delhi, 1971), pl. I. 1. For the information that these coins were found in the Punjab region by Alexander Cunningham, see George Macdonald, Ancient Greek (Athenian and Macedonian) Coins in India, Appendix to Chapter XV, in E J Rapson (ed), *The Cambridge History of India* 1, (reprint, Delhi, 1987), pp. 346-350, on pp. 347-348.

3 A K Narain, *The Indo-Greeks*, (Oxford, 1957), pp. 4-5.

of the second century BC.[1] But this date is believed to be somewhat late, for the *Hirañasame* coins of Takshaśilā, as seen above, served as the prototype for the *Hirañasame* coins of the Indo-Greek ruler, Agathokles (*circa* 180-165 BC). Alexander Cunningham would seem to refer these coins to the third century BC, as he regards the script of these pieces as Aśokan.[2] But E J Rapson places, at least the Dojaka-*nigama* coins,[3] at the beginning of the fourth century BC,[4] perhaps because, out of the Dojaka-*nigama* coins of Takshaśilā illustrated by John Allan, one has the Brāhmī legend in the reverse order,[5] which has been taken to point to an earlier date.

8. Thus, it would appear that these coins from Takshaśilā should be regarded as the earliest inscribed coins of India, instead of the inscribed coins of the *madhyadeśa* (like Eran, Kaushambi, etc), which seem to be datable to the second century BC.

From the above, it would seem that inscribed Greek coins were familiar in Afghanistan and northwestern India, and people of

---

1 John Allan, *Catalogue of the Coins of Ancient India, in the British Museum, London*, (London, 1936), pp.cxxvii-cxxviii.

2 Alexander Cunningham, *Coins of Ancient India*, (reprint, Varanasi, 1971), p. 63.

3 John Allan, *Catalogue of the Coins of Ancient India, in the British Museum, London*, (London, 1936), pl. XXXI. 2-4.

4 E J Rapson, *Indian Coins*, (Strassburg, 1897), pp. 4, 6.

5 John Allan, *Catalogue of the Coins of Ancient India, in the British Museum, London*, (London, 1936), pl. XXXI. 4.

these regions were not only imitating these inscribed coins, but were also, sometimes, introducing their tribal names on these imitation Greek coins, during the Achaemenian period. An Achaemenian satrap of the Punjab region struck coins, bearing his name, after the Greek fashion of inscribing coins. Therefore, it is not surprising that Indian inscribed coins appear, for the first time, at Takshaśilā in northwestern India, the region most prone to foreign influence, and not in the *madhyadeśa*. As seen above, the inscribed coins from the interior regions of India are, perhaps, later than the inscribed coins from Takshaśilā. Although John Allan has dated the Eran coins, bearing the legend, *Dhamapālasa*, to the third century BC,[1] and this has been accepted by a number of scholars, I would like to point out that the Eran region was under the Mauryas in the third century BC, and it is a well-known fact that these Mauryas were ardent believers in a strong centralized government. Is it possible that, in the third century BC, during the rule of the Mauryas, there existed some local king at Eran, who was issuing coins bearing his own name ? As there is not much possibility of this, these coins would have to be placed somewhat later, perhaps in the second century BC. The same cannot be argued against dating the inscribed coins from Takshaśilā to the third century BC, as they were not issued by any king, but by *nigamas*.[2]

1 John Allan, *Catalogue of the Coins of Ancient India, in the British Museum, London*, (London, 1936), p. 140.

2 Economic organizations. See Georg Bühler, *Indian Studies* 3, (2nd ed), (Strassburg, 1898), p. 49; Alexander Cunningham, *Archaeological Survey Reports* 14, p. 20; John Allan, *Catalogue of the Coins of Ancient India, in the British Museum, London*, (London, 1936), p. cxxvi. But D R Bhandarkar, *Carmichael Lectures on Ancient Indian Numismatics*, (reprint, Patna, 1984), pp. 174-178, regards them as townships.

Then, there is also the view of E J Rapson,[1] that some of the inscribed *negama* coins from Takshaśilā might belong to even the beginning of the fourth century BC, as seen earlier, much before the rise of the Mauryas.

K P Jayaswal has tried to read the initials of the names of some Maurya emperors on some punch-marked coins from Magadha.[2] Some scholars regard the symbols on punch-marked coins as pictographs, and have tried to decipher them by adopting the *Tāntrika bījamantra* system.[3] But both these attempts to regard punch-marked coins as inscribed money do not seem to be based on solid ground,[4] and, as such, these punch-marked coins from the *madhyadeśa* cannot be regarded as the earliest inscribed monetary issues of India.

It is, therefore, likely that the ancient Indians, like the Achaemenians, started inscribing their coins under Greek influence.[5]

1 E J Rapson, *Indian Coins*, (Strassburg, 1897), pp. 4, 6.

2 *Proceedings of the Annual Meeting of the Numismatic Society of India*, 1935, pp. 11ff.

3 See Swami Sankarananda, Legends on Punch-marked Coins, *Journal of the Numismatic Society of India* 12(1), (1950), pp. 11-25.

4 See Jaiprakash, On Ancient Indian Coin-legends, *Journal of the Numismatic Society of India* 23, (1961), pp. 241-258, on pp. 242-244.

5 Prashant Srivastava, The Beginning of Legends on Ancient India Coins, *Purāvṛitta—Journal of the Department of Ancient Indian History and Archaeology, University of Lucknow* 1, (2000-2001), pp. 215-220.

5

Some problems of attribution

Sometimes, numismatists face problems in the attribution of coins. For instance, there are a number of Sātavāhana rulers, whose names occurs in the puranic lists, but their coins are not available. But problem arises, when numismatists are faced with coins of Sātavāhana rulers, whose names do not occur in the puranic lists. Then, there might be more than one rulers, bearing the same name. But the most vexing problems are presented by coins, bearing names of rulers, who are not known from any other source.

Sophytes. This king is known to have issued two types of coins. The first type has, on the obverse, the head of the king, wearing 'an Attic helmet ornamented with a laurel wreath, and a cheek-piece with a bird's wing', to the right; the reverse has a cock to the right, and the legend, *Sophytou* (coins no. 17, 18).[1] The second type has the head of Athena, wearing a Corinthian helmet, to the right, on the obverse,

---

1 Osmund Bopearachchi and Wilfried Pieper, *Ancient Indian Coins*, (Brepols, Turnhout, 1998), p. 192.

while the reverse is similar to that of the first type.[1] Both the types have the symbol, *caduceus*, on the reverse.

Alexander Cunningham, who published the first known coin in the name of this ruler, identified him with the Indian prince, Sopeithes, mentioned in classical sources as a contemporary of Alexander, and this identification was accepted by most of the writers on the subject.[2] Consequently, Sophytes was regarded as a ruler of the Salt Range in the Punjab.[3] However, R B Whitehead, who had earlier himself regarded Sophytes as a satrap in the Punjab region,[4] later on, on the basis of the *provenance* of his coins, placed him in the Oxus region,[5] and this has been accepted by all the subsequent writers on the subject; Osmund Bopearachchi is of the view that this is supported by the recent discoveries of coins and coin hoards in Afghanistan.[6] Cunningham proposes 312-306 BC as the date for Sophytes.[7] E J Rapson regarded

---

1 Osmund Bopearachchi and Wilfried Pieper, *Ancient Indian Coins*, (Brepols, Turnhout, 1998), p. 192.

2 Alexander Cunningham, Coins of the Indian Prince Sophytes, A Contemporary of Alexander the Great, *Numismatic Chronicle*, 1866, pp. 220-231, on pp. 221-222.

3 Alexander Cunningham, Coins of the Indian Prince Sophytes, A Contemporary of Alexander the Great, in Alexander Cunningham, *Coins of Alexander's Successors in the East*, (reprint, Varanasi, 1970), p. 5.

4 R B Whitehead, *Catalogue of the Coins in the Punjab Museum, Lahore* 1, The Indo-Greek Coins, (Oxford, 1914), p. 9.

5 R B Whitehead, The Eastern Satrap Sophytes, *Numismatic Chronicle*, 1943, pp. 60-72, on p. 72.

6 Osmund Bopearachchi and Wilfried Pieper, *Ancient Indian Coins*, (Brepols, Turnhout, 1998), p. 189.

7 Alexander Cunningham, Coins of the Indian Prince Sophytes, A Contemporary of Alexander the Great, in Alexander Cunningham,

the coins of Sophytes as older than those of Seleukos I and contemporaneous with Alexander,[1] and Whitehead also places them as early as 320 BC.[2] Narain regards Sophytes as 'an eastern satrap under Achaemenid rule, a Greek with the semblance of an Iranian name', and is of the view that these coins were struck prior to the invasion of India by Alexander.[3]

But, according to some scholars, the coins of Sophytes, which are directly linked with one type showing the head of Zeus on the obverse,[4] and, thus, similar to the coins issued by Philip and Alexander in Macedonia,[5] are nearer to the coins of Seleukos I minted in Bactria, a fact also remarked by scholars like Percy Gardner,[6] V A Smith,[7] and B V Head,[8] and this has led to the suggestion that he was ruling, not only at the time of the invasion of India by Alexander, but also

---

Coins of Alexander's Successors in the East, (reprint, Varanasi, 1970), p. 3.

1 E J Rapson, *Ancient India, from the Earliest Times to the First Century AD*, (London, 1914), pp. 152-153.

2 R B Whitehead, The Eastern Satrap Sophytes, *Numismatic Chronicle*, 1943, pp. 60-72, on p. 72.

3 A K Narain, *The Indo-Greeks*, (Oxford, 1957), pp. 4-5.

4 Osmund Bopearachchi and Wilfried Pieper, *Ancient Indian Coins*, (Brepols, Turnhout, 1998), p. 192.

5 Osmund Bopearachchi and Wilfried Pieper, *Ancient Indian Coins*, (Brepols, Turnhout, 1998), p. 194.

6 Percy Gardner, *Catalogue of the Coins of the Greek and Scythic Kings of Bactria and India, in the British Museum, London*, (reprint, New Delhi, 1971), p. xx.

7 V A Smith, *Coins of Ancient India—Catalogue of the Coins in the Indian Museum, Calcutta, including the Cabinet of the Asiatic Society of Bengal* 1, (reprint, Varanasi, 1972), p. 7, n. 1.

8 B V Head, The Earliest Graeco-Bactrian and Graeco-Indian Coins, *Numismatic Chronicle*, 1906, pp. 1-16, on p. 13.

during the eastern expedition of Seleukos I.[1] On this basis, von Sallet suggested 306 BC as the date for the Sophytes coins,[2] while Smith placed them in 305 BC.[3] The coins of Sophytes are linked, geographically and chronologically, to the 'owls' and 'eagles' by *provenance*, stylistic features, symbols, attributes, and die-adjustment.[4] Besides, a type of Sophytes, bearing the bust of Athena, wearing the Corinthian helmet, to the right, on the obverse, is derived from the gold coins of Alexander.[5] A similar coin for Egypt (?) bears the Egyptian hieroglyph *uah* in the place where the name of Sophytes occurs on his coins, and E T Newell says that this coin from Egypt is copied from the gold *staters* of Alexander or his immediate successors.[6] Hence, according to Osmund Bopearachchi, Sophytes cannot be placed before Alexander's

---

1 Percy Gardner, *Catalogue of the Coins of the Greek and Scythic Kings of Bactria and India, in the British Museum, London*, (reprint, New Delhi, 1971), p. xx; V A Smith, *Coins of Ancient India—Catalogue of the Coins in the Indian Museum, Calcutta, including the Cabinet of the Asiatic Society of Bengal* 1, (reprint, Varanasi, 1972), p. 7, n. 1.

2 A von Sallet, *Die Nachfolger Alexanders des Grossen in Baktrien und Indien* 2, Die Münzen, *Zeitschrift für Numismatik* 6, pp. 271-411, on p. 285.

3 V A Smith, *Coins of Ancient India—Catalogue of the Coins in the Indian Museum, Calcutta, including the Cabinet of the Asiatic Society of Bengal* 1, (reprint, Varanasi, 1972), p. 7, n. 1.

4 Osmund Bopearachchi and Wilfried Pieper, *Ancient Indian Coins*, (Brepols, Turnhout, 1998), pp. 192-193.

5 Osmund Bopearachchi and Wilfried Pieper, *Ancient Indian Coins*, (Brepols, Turnhout, 1998), p. 194.

6 E T Newell, *Miscellanea Numismatics—Cyrene to India*, Numismatic Notes and Monographs of the American Numismatic Society 82, (New York, 1937), pp. 59-60.

invasion, as suggested by Narain.[1] Bopearachchi is of the view that as the coins of Sophytes are copied from those of Seleukos I struck after his eastern expedition c 305 BC, these coins should be dated towards the close of the fourth century BC.[2] But the view of Narain cannot, altogether be ruled out.

Azes. A large number of coins bearing the name of Azes have come to the light. From the fact that, on some coins, the name of Azes occurs in Greek on the obverse, and of Azilises (Ayalisha) in Kharoshṭhī on the reverse,[3] while on some others, the order is reversed,[4] it has been suggested that there were two Śaka-Pahlava kings bearing the name Azes. Of these, the elder, that is Azes I, associated his son, Azilises, in government, perhaps in his old age, and the latter, in his turn, associated his own son, Azes II, in government towards the close of his reign.[5] The issue of the existence of

---

1 Osmund Bopearachchi and Wilfried Pieper, *Ancient Indian Coins*, (Brepols, Turnhout, 1998), p. 195.

2 Osmund Bopearachchi and Wilfried Pieper, *Ancient Indian Coins*, (Brepols, Turnhout, 1998), pp. 195-196.

3 Percy Gardner, *Catalogue of the Coins of the Greek and Scythic Kings of Bactria and India, in the British Museum, London*, (reprint, New Delhi, 1971), pl. XXXII. 9.

4 Alexander Cunningham, *Coins of the Indo-Scythian, Sakas, Kushans*, (reprint, Varanasi, 1971), pl. VII. A2; Percy Gardner, *Catalogue of the Coins of the Greek and Scythic Kings of Bactria and India, in the British Museum, London*, (reprint, New Delhi, 1971), pl. XXI. 5.

5 E J Rapson, The Scythian and Parthian Invaders, Chapter XXIII, in E J Rapson (ed), *The Cambridge History of India* 1, (reprint, Delhi, 1987), pp. 508-536, on p. 516; H H Wilson, *Ariana Antiqua—A Descriptive Account of the Antiquities and Coins of Afghanistan*, (reprint, Delhi, 1971), p. 319; John H Marshall, *Taxila* 1, (reprint,

two kings named Azes is a contentious one, and needs to be addressed in some detail, as it has a bearing on the history and coinage of the Śaka-Pahlava rulers.

R B Whitehead, on the contrary, is of the view that there might have been two kings named Azilises, and only one Azes. His argument is that as the 'best didrachms of Azes compare unfavourably with the fine silver coins of Azilises', hence, Azilises preceded Azes.[1] However, in view of the fact that the coins of Azilises do not show any great difference in style and execution, while the same cannot be said of the coins bearing the name of Azes, there is greater likelihood of there being two rulers named Azes. Scholars like Ernst Herzfeld[2] and J E van Lohuizen de Leeuw[3] suggested that Azes, Azilises, Aya, and Ayilisha (the last two being the Prakrit forms of Azes and Azilises, respectively) are the different names of one and the same king. But this view has not been taken seriously by scholars. Sten Konow was earlier of the view that there was only one Azes.[4] But later

---

Delhi, 1975), p. 53; W W Tarn, *The Greeks in Bactria and India*, (reprint, New Delhi, 1980), p. 348; etc.

1 R B Whitehead, *Catalogue of the Coins in the Punjab Museum, Lahore* 1, The Indo-Greek Coins, (Oxford, 1914), p. 93.

2 Ernst Herzfeld, *Sakastan*, (Berlin, 1932), pp. 197-198.

3 J E van Lohuizen de Leeuw, *The "Scythian" Period*, (Leiden, 1949). See Prashant Srivastava, *Encyclopaedia of Indian Coins (Ancient Coins of Northern India, up to* circa *650 AD)* 1, (Delhi, 2012), pp. 58-60.

4 Sten Konow, *Corpus Inscriptionum Indicarum*, 2(1), Kharoshṭhī Inscriptions with the Exception of those of Aśoka, (Calcutta, 1929), p. XL.

on, he accepted the theory of the existence of two kings named Azes.[1]

Jenkins has shown that some coins bearing the name of Azes are of fine quality silver, bear the obverse device of horseman king with spear, and have the early form of the Kharoshṭhī letter *sa* in the reverse legend; other coins bearing the name of Azes are in debased silver, bear the obverse device of horseman king with whip, and have the late form of the Kharoshṭhī letter *sa*. He ascribes the former coins to Azes I, and the latter to Azes II.[2] R C Senior has recently pleaded the case for a single king named Azes.[3] He regards all the joint issues in the name of Azes/Azilises or Azilises/Azes as 'mules'. He says that 'mules', by their very nature, are extremely rare, while joint coins should be more prolific and produced from several dies. But he himself admits that the Azilises/Azes copper coins are 'more problematic since more than one die is known and so far no coin exists with an Azes obverse (ie, no coin of this type known of Azes alone)'.[4] He has tried to explain away this problem by suggesting a number of possibilities and 'unusual' situations.[5] The evidence of coin hoards, too, has been cited,[6]

1 Sten Konow, Notes on Indo-Scythian Chronology, *Journal of Indian History* 12, (1933), pp. 1ff, on p. 24.

2 G K Jenkins, Indo-Scythic Mints, *Journal of the Numismatic Society of India* 17(2), (1955), pp. 1-26, and plates.

3 R C Senior, Gondophares-Sases, St Thomas and the Era of Kanishka, *Numismatic Studies* 6, (2001), pp. 59-121, on pp. 80-85.

4 R C Senior, Gondophares-Sases, St Thomas and the Era of Kanishka, *Numismatic Studies* 6, (2001), pp. 59-121, on p. 84.

5 R C Senior, Gondophares-Sases, St Thomas and the Era of Kanishka, *Numismatic Studies* 6, (2001), pp. 59-121, on p. 85.

6 R C Senior, Gondophares-Sases, St Thomas and the Era of Kanishka, *Numismatic Studies* 6, (2001), pp. 59-121, on pp. 86-106.

but it cannot be said to be conclusive. For instance, the Nul Guniar hoard, which has coins of both the 'King mounted with spear' and 'King mounted with whip' types of Azes, but no coins of Azilises, has been taken as confirmation of the suggestion that Azilises did not intervene between Azes I and Azes II series of coins. It is further argued that all the coins were patinated to the same extent, showing that they were deposited 'within a short period of issue'.[1] But should such conclusions be drawn on the basis of a hoard of mere 11 coins ? Would the patination become markedly different within a period of, say, some 20 years ?

The stratified evidence of the Azes coins from Takshaśilā also supports the existence of two kings bearing the name of Azes.[2] The occurrence of the early form of the Kharoshṭhī letter *sa* on the coins of Azes found in the lower strata, when compared with the occurrence of the later form of the same letter on the Azes coins from the upper strata, also indicates the existence of two Azes.[3] Moreover, the coins of Azilises themselves show no debasement, and, as such, the debased coins of Azes [II] cannot be placed before him.[4] The view of R C Senior, that Azilises started ruling at the same time as Azes, and predeceased the latter,[5] is difficult to accept.

---

1 R C Senior, Gondophares-Sases, St Thomas and the Era of Kanishka, *Numismatic Studies* 6, (2001), pp. 59-121, on p. 90.

2 John H Marshall, *Taxila* 1, (reprint, Delhi, 1975), p. 131.

3 N G Majumdar, Notes on the Coins of Azes, *Archaeological Survey of India—Annual Report*, 1928-1929, pp. 169-174.

4 B N Mukherjee, *An Agrippan Source—A Study in Indo-Parthian History*, (Calcutta, 1969), pp. 86-87.

5 R C Senior, Gondophares-Sases, St Thomas and the Era of Kanishka, *Numismatic Studies* 6, (2001), pp. 59-121, on p. 112.

But the most clinching evidence in favour of the existence of two kings named Azes is as follows : The dates of Vijayamitra are available from several inscriptions. The Shinkot-Bajaur relic-casket inscriptions refer to his regnal year 5.[1] Then, there is the Indravarman reliquary inscription of Azes year 63, which mentions year 25 of Vijayamitra.[2] A third inscription, the Prahodia inscription, is reported to refer to year 32 of Vijayamitra,[3] and this may be the reason for identifying *apracharaja* whose regnal year 25 is mentioned in the Indravarman reliquary inscription, with Vijayamitra. Finally, there is the so-called 'Bhagamoya' inscription of year 77 of Azes, which also mentions Vijayamitra.[4] If Azes year 63 of the Indravarman relic-casket inscription, is regnal year 25 of Vijayamitra, then Azes year 77 of the 'Bhagamoya' inscription will make regnal year 39 of Vijayamitra. This shows that Vijayamitra must have ruled for 39+ years.

The era of Azes is generally identified with Vikrama *saṁvat* commencing 58 BC.[5] On this basis, year 63 of Azes, mentioned in the Indravarman relic casket inscription, comes to 5 AD. This is believed to be the 25th regnal year of

1 N G Majumdar, The [Shinkot] Bajaur Casket Kharoshṭhī Inscriptions of the Reign of Menander, *Epigraphia India* 24, (1937-1938), pp. 1-8.

2 H W Bailey, Two Kharoṣṭhī Inscriptions from Avaca, *Journal of the Royal Asiatic Society of Great Birtian and Ireland*, (1978), no. 1, pp. 3-13, on pp. 3-4.

3 Akira Sadakata, The Prahodia Inscription of Vijayamitra, year 32, *Eastern*, 1991, Tokai University.

4 H W Bailey, Two Kharoṣṭhī Inscriptions, (1982), *Journal of the Royal Asiatic Society of Great Birtian and Ireland*, (1982), no. 2, pp. 142ff, on pp. 149-155.

5 R C Senior, Gondophares-Sases, St Thomas and the Era of Kanishka, *Numismatic Studies* 6, (2001), pp. 59-121, on p. 75.

Vijayamitra. Hence, Vijayamitra would have started ruling *c* 20 BC. The 'Bhagamoya' inscription shows that he was ruling in Azes year 77, ie, 19 AD. We have joint coins to show that Azes had Indravasu, the son of Vijayamitra, as his subordinate ruler,[1] and Aśpavarman, the son of Vijayamitra's nephew, Indravarman,[2] as his *strategos*. If there were only one Azes, this would mean that he survived, not only Vijayamitra, but also received the services of Vijayamitra's son, Indravasu, and of Aśpavarman, the son of Vijayamitra's nephew, Indravarman. According to the 'Bhagamoya' inscription, Vijayamitra was ruling in Azes year 77. To have Aśpavarman serve under him, Azes would require an exceptionally long reign of 77+ years. But if we accept the existence of two kings named Azes, this problem would be solved. We would have an Azes whose year is mentioned in these records, and a second king of that name as overlord of Indravasu and Aśpavarman. Azes I would have been dead at the time of the issue of the Indravarman reliquary inscription of Azes year 63 (= 5 AD), for this epigraph refers to the era as *maharajasa Ayasa atidasa*, 'of the *Maharaja* Aya deceased'.[3] It is quite possible that Azes I was not alive even in the early years of the reign of Vijayamitra. R C

---

1 B N Mukherjee, *An Agrippan Source—A Study in Indo-Parthian History*, (Calcutta, 1969), p. 88, and pl. III. 14.

2 Percy Gardner, *Catalogue of the Coins of the Greek and Scythic Kings of Bactria and India, in the British Museum, London*, (reprint, New Delhi, 1971), pl. XX. 2.

3 H W Bailey, Two Kharoṣṭhī Inscriptions from Avaca, *Journal of the Royal Asiatic Society of Great Birtian and Ireland*, (1978), no. 1, pp. 3-13, on pp. 3, 10.

Senior seems to be right, when he suggests,[1] on numismatic grounds, that Vijayamitra asserted himself immediately after the death of Azes, *c* 20 BC.[2]

V'ima Takshuma. Earlier, on the basis of the available evidence, it was believed by most of the scholars that, among the Kushāṇas, there was only one ruler with V'ima as his forename, namely V'ima Kadphises, and he was regarded as the son and successor of Kujula Kadphises.[3] However, in recent years, epigraphic and numismatic evidence (coin no. 19) has been forthcoming to suggest that, besides V'ima Kadphises, there was another Kushāṇa ruler, who had V'ima as his forename, but the last component of his name, as known from coins and inscriptions, has been read variously by scholars, like G Fussman, Nicholas Sims-Williams and Joe Cribb, R C Senior, B N Mukherjee, and Heinrich Lüders,

---

1 R C Senior, The Apracharajas and their Coinage, *Numismatic Digest* 20, (1996), pp. 33-40, on p. 36.

2 Prashant Srivastava, Two Śaka-Pahlava Kings Named Azes ? in A K Sinha (ed), *Dimensions in Indian History*, (New Delhi, 2005), pp. 74-79; Prashant Srivastava, *The Apracharajas—A History Based on Coins and Inscriptions*, (Delhi, 2007), Appendix I, pp. 79-84; Prashant Srivastava, *Encyclopaedia of Indian Coins*, I, (Delhi, 2012), pp. 58-60.

3 Eg, H C Raychaudhuri, *Political History of Ancient India, from the Accession of Parīkshit to the Extinction of the Gupta Dynasty* (7th ed, Calcutta, 1972), p. 409; D C Sircar, The Kushāṇas. Chapter IX in R C Majumdar, A D Pusalker, and A K Majumdar (ed), *The Age of Imperial Unity* (History and Culture of the Indian People 2, Bombay, 1980), pp. 136-153, on p. 139; B N Mukherjee, *An Agrippan Source—A Study in Indo-Parthian History*, (Calcutta, 1969), p. 217; Gritli von Mitterwallner, *Kuṣāṇa Coins and Kuṣāṇa Sculptures from Mathurā*, (Mathura, 1986), p. 2.

as *Takpio,*[1] *Takta,*[2] *Taktoo,*[3] *Takkashama,*[4] *Takshomo,*[5] or *Takshuma.*[6]

The epigraphic evidence for the existence of this ruler is in the form of at least three inscriptions, namely the Mat inscription, the Dasht-i-Nawur inscriptions, and the Rabatak inscription. Of these, the first is engraved between the feet of a seated royal statue discovered in the Kushāṇa *devakula* at Mat near Mathura.[7] The inscription, while mentioning the construction of a temple, a garden, a tank,

---

1 G Fussman, *Documents Épigraphiques Kouchans, "I. –Inscriptions et Antiquités du Dašt-e Nāwur", Bulletin de l'Ecole Française d'Extreme-Orient* 61 (1974), pp. 2-50, on p. 18.

2 Nicholas Sims-Williams and Joe Cribb, A New Bactrian Inscription of Kanishka the Great, *Silk Road Art and Archaeology* 4 (1995-1996), The Institute of Silk Road Studies, Kamakura, pp. 75-142, on pp. 98, 142.

3 Nicholas Sims-Williams and Joe Cribb, A New Bactrian Inscription of Kanishka the Great, *Silk Road Art and Archaeology* 4 (1995-1996), The Institute of Silk Road Studies, Kamakura, pp. 75-142, on p. 95.

4 R C Senior, *Indo-Scythian Coins and History* 1, (London, 2001), p. 210.

5 B N Mukherjee, *Mathura and its Society—The Śaka-Pahlava Phase*, (Calcutta, 1981), p. 43.

6 Heinrich Lüders, *Mathura Inscriptions*, edited by K L Janert, (Gottingen, 1961), p, 135; Gritli von Mitterwallner, *Kuṣāṇa Coins and Kuṣāṇa Sculptures from Mathurā*, (Mathura, 1986), pp. 54ff; B N Mukherjee, Vima Taktu, An Alleged Kushana King, *Numismatic Digest* 21-22 (1997-1998), pp. 5-10, on p. 6ff; Michael Mitchiner, The Kushan King, Vima Takshuma, Son of Kujula Kadphises: A Discussion of his Name, *Numismatic Digest* 25-26 (2001-2002), pp. 43-50, on pp. 45, 48.

7 Heinrich Lüders, *Mathura Inscriptions*, edited by K L Janert, (Gottingen, 1961), p. 135; J M Rosenfeld, *The Dynastic Arts of the Kushans*, (Berkeley and Los Angeles, 1967), pp. 144-145, and figure

a well, an assembly hall, and a gateway, refers to V[e]ma Ta[kshu]ma, who is called *mahārāja rājātirāja devaputra Kushāṇaputra shāhi*. The medial sign with the letter *va* in the forename of the king is not clear, and the forename has been read variously as *Vama-*,[1] *Vema*,[2] *V[e]ma*,[3] *V[e]mo*,[4] or *Vimo*.[5] Though the compound character following *ta* in the surname is not very clear,[6] the full surname has been read as *Takshuma* by most of the scholars,[7] but B N Mukherjee

---

1; Gritli von Mitterwallner, *Kuṣāṇa Coins and Kuṣāṇa Sculptures from Mathurā*, (Mathura, 1986) pp. 53ff, and pls. 1 and 2.

1 J Ph Vogel, Explorations at Mathurā : a. Excavations at Mat. *Archaeological Survey of India—Annual Report*, 1911-1912, pp. 120-133, on p. 124.

2 K P Jayaswal, The Statue of Wema Kadphises and Kushan Chronology, *Journal of the Bihar and Orissa Research Society* 6 (1920), pp. 12-22, on p. 13; J M Rosenfeld, *The Dynastic Arts of the Kushans*, (Indian edition, New Delhi, 1993), p. 144.

3 Gritli von Mitterwallner, *Kuṣāṇa Coins and Kuṣāṇa Sculptures from Mathurā*, (Mathura, 1986), p. 56; Rosenfeld, *The Dynastic Arts of the Kushans*, (Indian edition, New Delhi, 1993), p. 299n.

4 Heinrich Lüders, *Mathura Inscriptions*, edited by K L Janert, (Gottingen, 1961), p. 135n.

5 B N Mukherjee, *The Kushāṇa Genealogy*, (Calcutta, 1967), p. 99n.

6 Michael Mitchiner, The Kushan King, Vima Takshuma, Son of Kujula Kadphises : A Discussion of his Name, *Numismatic Digest* 25-26 (2001-2002), pp. 43-50, on p. 48.

7 Heinrich Lüders, *Mathura Inscriptions*, edited by K L Janert, (Gottingen, 1961), p. 135; Gritli von Mitterwallner, *Kuṣāṇa Coins and Kuṣāṇa Sculptures from Mathurā*, (Mathura, 1986), p. 55ff; Michael Mitchiner, The Kushan King, Vima Takshuma, Son of Kujula Kadphises : A Discussion of his Name, *Numismatic Digest* 25-26 (2001-2002), pp. 43-50, on p. 48; B N Mukherjee, *The Kushāṇa Genealogy*, (Calcutta, 1967), p. 57.

has suggested that it may also be read as *Tākshuma*.[1] The difference between the Brāhmī and the Kharoshṭhī forms of the surname might be due to the absence of long vowels in the latter script.[2] Interestingly, in line 2 of the inscription, V[e] ma Takshuma is called *Kushāṇaputro*. The *Kushāṇa* in this word is regarded as 'identical with the *Guṣaṇa* or *Khuṣaṇa*, mentioned without personal name' in the Panjtar inscription of the year 122,[3] and the Taxila silver scroll inscription of the year 136,[4] respectively, who is generally identified with Kujula Kadphises.[5] If this identification be correct, the Mat inscription also gives the relationship between Kujula Kadphises and V'ima Takshuma as that of father and son.

Five inscriptions, two in Graeco-Bactrian, two in Kharoshṭhī, and one in 'an unknown script (and language ?)', were discovered on a peak of Mount Qarabayu to the west of Dasht-i-Nawur in Afghanistan.[6] The Graeco-Bactrian

1 B N Mukherjee, *Mathura and its Society—The Śaka-Pahlava Phase*, (Calcutta, 1981), pp. 42-43; B N Mukherjee, Vima Taktu, An Alleged Kushana King, *Numismatic Digest* 21-22 (1997-1998), pp. 5-10, on p. 6.

2 B N Mukherjee, Vima Taktu, An Alleged Kushana King, *Numismatic Digest* 21-22 (1997-1998), pp. 5-10, on p. 9.

3 Sten Konow, *Corpus Inscriptionum Indicarum* 2(1), Kharoshṭhī Inscriptions with the Exceptions of those of Aśoka, (Calcutta, 1929), pp. 67-70.

4 Sten Konow, *Corpus Inscriptionum Indicarum* 2(1), Kharoshṭhī Inscriptions with the Exceptions of those of Aśoka, (Calcutta, 1929), pp. 70-77.

5 Gritli von Mitterwallner, *Kuṣāṇa Coins and Kuṣāṇa Sculptures from Mathurā*, (Mathura, 1986), p. 59n.

6 G Fussman, *Documents Épigraphiques Kouchans, "I. –Inscriptions et Antiquités du Dašt-e Nāwur"*, *Bulletin de l'Ecole Française d'Extreme-Orient* 61 (1974), pp. 2-50; G Djelani Davary and Helmut

inscription, no. 1, in line 3, refers to *Ooemo Tak[..]o*,[1] while a Kharoshṭhī inscription refers to the reign of Vhama Kuśa.[2] B N Mukherjee[3] feels that it is 'impossible to be sure of any reading' of the second part of the name in the Graeco-Bactrian version 'beyond *Tak*', but he had earlier restored it as *Takshomo*.[4] It is believed that the occasion for the engraving of the Graeco-Bactrian inscription, no. 1, at Dasht-i-Nawur was the first visit of V'ima Takshuma to that site.[5]

Humbach, *Die Baktrische Inschrift IDN 1 von Dasht-e Nāwūr (Afghanistan), Akademie der Wissenschaften und der Literatur, Abhandlungen der Geistes- und Sozialwissenschaftlichen Klasse*, Jahrgang 1976, Nr. 1 (Wiesbaden), (1976), pp. 3-21; Gritli von Mitterwallner, *Kuṣāṇa Coins and Kuṣāṇa Sculptures from Mathurā*, (Mathura, 1986), pp. 57-59.

1 G Fussman, *Documents Épigraphiques Kouchans, "I. –Inscriptions et Antiquités du Dašt-e Nāwur", Bulletin de l'Ecole Française d'Extreme-Orient* 61 (1974), pp. 2-50, pl. XV; G Djelani Davary and Helmut Humbach, *Die Baktrische Inschrift IDN 1 von Dasht-e Nāwūr (Afghanistan), Akademie der Wissenschaften und der Literatur, Abhandlungen der Geistes- und Sozialwissenschaftlichen Klasse*, Jahrgang 1976, Nr. 1 (Wiesbaden), (1976), pp. 3-21; Gritli von Mitterwallner, *Kuṣāṇa Coins and Kuṣāṇa Sculptures from Mathurā*, (Mathura, 1986), p. 58.

2 G Fussman, *Documents Épigraphiques Kouchans, "I. –Inscriptions et Antiquités du Dašt-e Nāwur", Bulletin de l'Ecole Française d'Extreme-Orient* 61 (1974), pp. 2-50, on p. 22; B N Mukherjee, Vima Taktu, An Alleged Kushana King, *Numismatic Digest* 21-22 (1997-1998), pp. 5-10, on p. 5.

3 B N Mukherjee, Vima Taktu, An Alleged Kushana King, *Numismatic Digest* 21-22 (1997-1998), pp. 5-10, on pp. 5-6.

4 B N Mukherjee, *Mathura and its Society—The Śaka-Pahlava Phase*, (Calcutta, 1981), pp. 43, 44, 45.

5 G Djelani Davary and Helmut Humbach, *Die Baktrische Inschrift IDN 1 von Dasht-e Nāwūr (Afghanistan), Akademie der Wissenschaften und der Literatur, Abhandlungen der Geistes- und*

The recently discovered Rabatak (Baghlan) inscription, from northern Afghanistan,[1] is of great significance for the study of Kushāṇa history.[2] It is observed that the inscription 'seems to have cleared up the mystery of Kujula Kadphises' successor even if it has left some doubt as to his true name'.[3] In lines 11 to 14, this Graeco-Bactrian inscription refers to the construction of certain divine images for the *devakula*, for the merit of four generations of Kushāṇa kings—Kanishka [I], and his father, grandfather, and great-grandfather, who are all mentioned by name, followed by the title of *shao* in each case. The names of Kanishka [I] (*Kaneshko*), his father V'ima Kadphises (*Ooemo Kadphiso*), and great-grandfather Kujula Kadphises (*Kozoulo Kadphiso*), are quite clear. But the left side of the rock, on which the inscription is engraved, is badly damaged, and, consequently, the name of

---

Sozialwissenschaftlichen Klasse, Jahrgang 1976, Nr. 1 (Wiesbaden), (1976), pp. 3-21, on p. 20, and n. 31; *cf* Gritli von Mitterwallner, *Kuṣāṇa Coins and Kuṣāṇa Sculptures from Mathurā*, (Mathura, 1986), p. 58.

1 Nicholas Sims-Williams and Joe Cribb, A New Bactrian Inscription of Kanishka the Great, *Silk Road Art and Archaeology* 4 (1995-1996), The Institute of Silk Road Studies, Kamakura, pp. 75-142; B N Mukherjee, The Great Kushāṇa Testament, *Indian Museum Bulletin* 30, (Calcutta, 1995); D W MacDowall, The Rabatak Inscription and the Nameless Kushan King, in *Cairo to Kabul : Afghan and Islamic Studies Presented to Ralph Pinder-Wilson* (London, 2002), pp. 163-169.

2 Editors' note on B N Mukherjee, Vima Taktu, An Alleged Kushana King, *Numismatic Digest* 21-22 (1997-1998), pp. 5-10, on p. 5.

3 R C Senior, *Indo-Scythian Coins and History* 1, (London, 2001), p. 210.

Kanishka's grandfather in line 13 is not fully legible.[1] The first two characters of the forename are lost; they seem to be followed by the Greek character *eta*; the *mu* following it is quite preserved. But it can be restored on the basis of the Graeco-Bactrian version of the Dasht-i-Nawur inscription,[2] where the forename seems to be *Ooemo*; the Prakrit version of the inscription has *Vhama* as the forename;[3] the Kharoshṭhī legends on coins ascribed to him clearly have *Vema* as the forename (below). As regards the surname of the grandfather of Kanishka I in the Rabatak inscription, the first character is lost; this is followed by an *alpha* and a *kappa*; the fourth character is again not legible; the surname definitely ends in double *omikron*. The first character can be restored as a *tau* on the basis of the Graeco-Bactrian version of the Dasht-i-Nawur inscription,[4] as also the Greek legend on the coins ascribed to him (below); the surname Tākshuma in the Mat inscription[5] also begins with *ta*. The fourth character has, again, been read as a *tau* by Sims-Williams, who restores the surname

1 Nicholas Sims-Williams and Joe Cribb, A New Bactrian Inscription of Kanishka the Great, *Silk Road Art and Archaeology* 4 (1995-1996), The Institute of Silk Road Studies, Kamakura, pp. 75-142, on p. 135, figure 6.

2 G Fussman, *Documents Épigraphiques Kouchans, "I. –Inscriptions et Antiquités du Dašt-e Nāwur", Bulletin de l'Ecole Française d'Extreme-Orient* 61 (1974), pp. 2-50, pl. XV.

3 G Fussman, *Documents Épigraphiques Kouchans, "I. –Inscriptions et Antiquités du Dašt-e Nāwur", Bulletin de l'Ecole Française d'Extreme-Orient* 61 (1974), pp. 2-50, on p. 22.

4 G Fussman, *Documents Épigraphiques Kouchans, "I. –Inscriptions et Antiquités du Dašt-e Nāwur", Bulletin de l'Ecole Française d'Extreme-Orient* 61 (1974), pp. 2-50, pl. XV.

5 Heinrich Lüders, *Mathura Inscriptions*, edited by K L Janert, (Gottingen, 1961), p. 135.

of Kanishka's grandfather as *Taktoo*.[1] Senior[2] proposes *Takkushama* as an alternative reading. But Mitchiner[3] feels that the traces of strokes, which can be seen in the Rabatak inscription, seem to suggest that the fourth character should be restored as a *zeta*, instead of a *tau*, and this restoration is apparently supported by the Dasht-i-Nawur inscription. He, thus, reads the name of Kanishka's grandfather in the Rabatak inscription as *Ooemo Takzoo*, which he finds 'compatible' with the Kharoshṭhī form *Takshuma* met with in the coin legends (below), and the Brāhmī form *Tākshuma* met with in the Mat inscription.[4] It may, incidentally, be mentioned that the Prakrit version of the Dasht-i-Nawur inscription has Kuśa as the surname of Vhama (= V'ima), obviously a contraction of the dynastic name, Kushāṇa.[5]

There are certain coins known from Kandahar and the Kabul valley, and from the region extending from Mathura

---

1 Nicholas Sims-Williams and Joe Cribb, A New Bactrian Inscription of Kanishka the Great, *Silk Road Art and Archaeology* 4 (1995-1996), The Institute of Silk Road Studies, Kamakura, pp. 75-142, on pp. 80, 95.

2 R C Senior, *Indo-Scythian Coins and History* 1, (London, 2001), p. 210.

3 Michael Mitchiner, The Kushan King, Vima Takshuma, Son of Kujula Kadphises : A Discussion of his Name, *Numismatic Digest* 25-26 (2001-2002), pp. 43-50, on p. 45.

4 Heinrich Lüders, *Mathura Inscriptions*, edited by K L Janert, (Gottingen, 1961), p. 135; B N Mukherjee, *The Kushāṇa Genealogy*, (Calcutta, 1967), p. 57; B N Mukherjee, Vima Taktu, An Alleged Kushana King, *Numismatic Digest* 21-22 (1997-1998), pp. 5-10, on p. 6n.

5 G Fussman, *Documents Épigraphiques Kouchans, "I. –Inscriptions et Antiquités du Dašt-e Nāwur"*, *Bulletin de l'Ecole Française d'Extreme-Orient* 61 (1974), pp. 2-50, on p. 22.

to Peshawar and into Russian Turkestan;[1] some coins are reported from as far east as Varanasi and Ghazipur in eastern Uttar Pradesh.[2] These coins bear only the epithets *Soter Megas*, and no personal name. These anonymous coins are struck in both base silver[3] or billon[4] and copper. The obverse of the base silver or billon coins has the equestrian king to the right, holding an *aṅkuśa* in his raised right hand, and the Greek legend *Basileos basileon soter megas*; the reverse has Zeus standing to the right, holding a sceptre in his left hand, and the Kharoshṭhī legend *Maharajasa rajatirajasa mahatasa tratarasa*. These coins have been associated with western Gandhāra.[5] The obverse of the copper coins, which have been associated with Mathura and southeastern Punjab, bears the diademed bust of the king to the right, while the reverse has Zeus standing to the left, holding a long sceptre

1 J M Rosenfeld, *The Dynastic Arts of the Kushans*, (Indian edition, New Delhi, 1993), p. 18.

2 Alexander Cunningham, Coins of the Kushans or Great Yue-ti. *Numismatic Chronicle* (3rd series) 12 (1892), pp. 40-82, on pp. 71-72; D W MacDowall, Soter Megas, The King of Kings, The Kushāṇa, *Journal of the Numismatic Society of India* 30 (1968), pp. 28-48, on p. 28.

3 Percy Gardner, *Catalogue of the Coins of the Greek and Scythic Kings of Bactria and India, In the British Museum, London*, (reprint, New Delhi, 1971), p. 114.

4 D W MacDowall, Soter Megas, The King of Kings, The Kushāṇa, *Journal of the Numismatic Society of India* 30 (1968), pp. 28-48, on p. 29.

5 Percy Gardner, *Catalogue of the Coins of the Greek and Scythic Kings of Bactria and India, In the British Museum, London*, (reprint, New Delhi, 1971), p. 114, and pl. XXIV. 1; D W MacDowall, Soter Megas, The King of Kings, The Kushāṇa, *Journal of the Numismatic Society of India* 30 (1968), pp. 28-48, on p. 29.

in his left hand, and a thunderbolt over an altar in his right hand; the reverse has the Greek legend *Basileos basileon soter megas*.[1] Then, there are some rare copper coins, which have been associated with the Kapiśā or Bactria region. These bear, on the obverse, the helmeted bust of the king, holding a spear, to the left; the reverse has the equestrian king to the right, holding an *aṅkuśa*, and the Greek legend *Basileos basileon soter megas*.[2] A large number of copper coins have the diademed and radiate bust of the king to the right, holding a long sceptre, on the obverse, and equestrian king to the right, holding an *aṅkuśa*, and the Greek legend *Basileos basileon soter megas*, on the reverse,[3] and this type is termed as the 'general coinage' of the issuer of these anonymous coins.[4]

---

1 Percy Gardner, *Catalogue of the Coins of the Greek and Scythic Kings of Bactria and India, In the British Museum, London*, (reprint, New Delhi, 1971), p. 116, and pl. XXIV. 5; D W MacDowall, Soter Megas, The King of Kings, The Kushāṇa, *Journal of the Numismatic Society of India* 30 (1968), pp. 28-48, on p. 30.

2 Percy Gardner, *Catalogue of the Coins of the Greek and Scythic Kings of Bactria and India, In the British Museum, London*, (reprint, New Delhi, 1971), p. 116, and pl. XXIV. 6; D W MacDowall, Soter Megas, The King of Kings, The Kushāṇa, *Journal of the Numismatic Society of India* 30 (1968), pp. 28-48, on pp. 30-31.

3 Percy Gardner, *Catalogue of the Coins of the Greek and Scythic Kings of Bactria and India, In the British Museum, London*, (reprint, New Delhi, 1971), pp. 114-115, and pl. XXIV. 2-4; D W MacDowall, Soter Megas, The King of Kings, The Kushāṇa, *Journal of the Numismatic Society of India* 30 (1968), pp. 28-48, on pp. 32-33.

4 D W MacDowall, Soter Megas, The King of Kings, The Kushāṇa, *Journal of the Numismatic Society of India* 30 (1968), pp. 28-48, on p. 32.

As to the identity of this issuer, some scholars proposed to regard him as a viceroy of V'ima Kadphises,[1] but the extensive distribution of this anonymous coinage (above) is 'fatal' to this theory.[2] Oikonomides takes *Soter* as a personal name on the analogy of the occurrence of *Soter* as a common name in the 'Hellenistic and Roman Near-East and Egypt', and regards him as 'the last of the Indo-Greek kings'.[3] Interpreting *sterossu*, occurring in the legend *Basileos sterosssu Hermaios* on some coins, believed to be posthumous issued in the name of Hermaios, as 'Soter Co-(regent) of', he proposes that King Soter first served as the 'co-regent' of Hermaios, and then accepted Kujula Kadphises, and finally V'ima Kadphises, as his sovereign. But this suggestion of Oikonomides is no longer acceptable in the light of the fact that the personal name of Soter Megas is now known to be Vi'ma Takshuma (below). M E Masson[4] pointed out some similarities between the anonymous coinage and the coinage

---

1 V A Smith, *The Early History of India*, (third revised and enlarged edition, reprint, New Delhi, 1999), p. 252n; D C Sircar, The Kushāṇas. Chapter IX in R C Majumdar, A D Pusalker, and A K Majumdar (ed), *The Age of Imperial Unity* (History and Culture of the Indian People 2, Bombay, 1980), pp. 136-153, on pp. 140-141; *cf* J M Rosenfeld, *The Dynastic Arts of the Kushans*, (Indian edition, New Delhi, 1993), p. 18.

2 D W MacDowall, Soter Megas, The King of Kings, The Kushāṇa, *Journal of the Numismatic Society of India* 30 (1968), pp. 28-48, on pp. 36-37.

3 Al N Oikonomides, Soter the Great—The Last of the Indo-Greek Kings, *Journal of the Numismatic Society of India* 35 (1973), pp. 82-89, on pp. 82-89.

4 *vide* D W MacDowall, Soter Megas, The King of Kings, The Kushāṇa, *Journal of the Numismatic Society of India* 30 (1968), pp. 28-48, on p. 38.

of Kujula Kadphises, and suggested that the coins with the 'non-personal inscriptions' might have been struck by Kujula Kadphises. But this suggestion has been rightly rejected by D W MacDowall.[1] MacDowall[2] points out the 'noticeable absence of any clear link in denomination or coin types' between the anonymous series and the coinage of Kujula Kadphises, and on this basis, he postulates a chronological break, in which he places the dynasty of Gondopharnes. According to him, this is supported by the excavations at Taxila, which reveal that after Kujula Kadphises, there ruled the dynasty of Gondopharnes, which was overthrown by the issuer of the anonymous coinage. He places Kujula Kadphises in the earlier decades of the first century AD, Gondopharnes in the middle of that century, and the issuer of the coins with the 'non-personal inscriptions' somewhat later. The anonymous coinage has Kushāṇa features, which proves that its issuer was a Kushāṇa ruler. MacDowall, however, feels that the Bactrian links of the issuer of this anonymous coinage 'reveal a very different crigin from Kujula Kadphises'. He, thus, regards the issuer of these coins as 'the founder of a new empire and a new dynasty', and responsible for 'the reconquest and consolidation of the Kushāṇa empire' in northwestern India. But this theory, too, is not acceptable in view of what follows. Cunningham[3] pointed

1 D W MacDowall, Soter Megas, The King of Kings, The Kushāṇa, *Journal of the Numismatic Society of India* 30 (1968), pp. 28-48, on p. 38.

2 D W MacDowall, Soter Megas, The King of Kings, The Kushāṇa, *Journal of the Numismatic Society of India* 30 (1968), pp. 28-48, on pp. 43-48.

3 Alexander Cunningham, Coins of the Śakas, *Numismatic Chronicle* (3rd series) 10 (1890), pp. 103-172, on pp. 114ff; Alexander

out several similarities between this anonymous coinage and the coins of V'ima Kadphises—both bear the titles *Basileos basileon soter megas*; both use the same peculiar form of the Kharoshṭhī letter *ja*; on some anonymous coins, the king holds a sceptre upright in front of his face, just as V'ima Kadphises is shown holding a club on some of his coins. Yet, the issuer of the anonymous coins should not be identified with V'ima Kadphises, because, despite of the similarities between the anonymous coinage and the coinage of V'ima Kadphises, there are some significant differences between the two.[1] V'ima Kadphises issued a copper coinage, which was 'remarkably uniform throughout all his territories'; on the contrary, besides the 'general coinage' (above), several types of the anonymous coins had 'a local circulation in different areas'. V'ima Kadphises struck all his coins on the Attic standard; most of the coins of the anonymous series are struck on the same standard, but the base silver/billon *tetradrachms* are struck on the Indian standard. Besides, V'ima Kadphises issued gold coins, but there are no gold coins in the anonymous series. No wonder, even after pointing out some similarities between the anonymous coinage and the coins of V'ima Kadphises, Cunningham[2] was still inclined to regard the issuer of the anonymous coinage and V'ima Kadphises as 'two princes', distinct from each other.

Cunningham, Coins of the Kushans or Great Yue-ti. *Numismatic Chronicle* (3rd series) 12 (1892), pp. 40-82, on pp. 71-72.

1 D W MacDowall, Soter Megas. The King of Kings, The Kushāṇa, *Journal of the Numismatic Society of India* 30 (1968), pp. 28-48, on p. 37.

2 Alexander Cunningham, Coins of the Kushans or Great Yue-ti. *Numismatic Chronicle* (3rd series) 12 (1892), pp. 40-82, on pp. 71-72.

As will be seen below, the coins of Classes I and II (below) apparently form a link between this anonymous coinage, and the coins of Class III (below) which clearly bear the name of V'ima Takshuma. This seems to show that the bulk of the coinage minted by the so-called 'nameless king *Soter Megas*',[1] was issued by none other than V'ima Takshuma.[2] It must be noted that Cunningham,[3] with his admirable and almost unerring foresight, included some coins with the Kharoshṭhī letter *vi* in the field, in the anonymous series.

Apart from these coins, there are three classes of coins,[4] which may be ascribed to V'ima Takshuma. The coins of Class I have the Kharoshṭhī character *vi* occupying a prominent place in the coins field, and are divided into three groups. The first group, linked with Bactria on the bases of the 'Attic' coin devices and the *provenance* of the coins, has the helmeted bust of the king and the character *vi* in the

1 Alexander Cunningham, Coins of the Śakas. *Numismatic Chronicle* (3rd series) 10 (1890), pp. 103-172, on pp. 114-115; D W MacDowall, Soter Megas, The King of Kings, The Kushāṇa, *Journal of the Numismatic Society of India* 30 (1968), pp. 28-48, on pp. 28-29.

2 Michael Mitchiner, The Kushan King, Vima Takṣhuma, Son of Kujula Kadphises : A Discussion of his Name, *Numismatic Digest* 25-26 (2001-2002), pp. 43-50, on p. 43.

3 Alexander Cunningham, Coins of the Śakas. *Numismatic Chronicle* (3rd series) 10 (1890), pp. 103-172, on p. 115.

4 D W MacDowall, Soter Megas, The King of Kings, The Kushāṇa, *Journal of the Numismatic Society of India* 30 (1968), pp. 28-48, on p. 31; Nicholas Sims-Williams and Joe Cribb, A New Bactrian Inscription of Kanishka the Great, *Silk Road Art and Archaeology* 4 (1995-1996), The Institute of Silk Road Studies, Kamakura, pp. 75-142, on pp. 115-116; R C Senior, *Indo-Scythian Coins and History* 2, (London, 2001), p. 221; Michael Mitchiner, The Kushan King, Vima Takshuma, Son of Kujula Kadphises : A Discussion of his Name, *Numismatic Digest* 25-26 (2001-2002), pp. 43-50, on pp. 45-47.

field on the obverse, and a horseman and the Greek legend *Basileos basileon soter megas* on the reverse. The second group, linked with northwestern India on the bases of the devices and the *provenance* of the coins, has the horseman and the Greek legend *Basileos basileon soter megas* on the obverse, and sceptre-bearing Zeus with the character *vi* and a flower vase in the field on the reverse. The third groups, linked with northwestern India and the previous groups on the bases of the flower vase and the *provenance* of the coins, has a standing male figure bearing a trident or sceptre and lion's skin and the character *vi* in the field on the obverse, and a standing goddess bearing *cornucopiae* with a flower vase and a *nandipada* in the field on the reverse; the legend is conspicuous by its absence. It has been suggested that the Kharoshṭhī character *vi* on these coins cannot be regarded as mint control mark, as they come from a wide geographical area spreading over Bactria and northwestern India; it should be taken as the abbreviated form of the personal name of the issuer, that is V'ima.[1] Class II consists of two coins, similar to the second group of Class I, with the difference that the Kharoshṭhī legend on these two coins is slightly longer with some extra characters at the end. On one of these coins,[2]

---

1 Alexander Cunningham, Coins of the Śakas. *Numismatic Chronicle* (3rd series) 10 (1890), pp. 103-172, on p. 115; Michael Mitchiner, The Kushan King, Vima Takshuma, Son of Kujula Kadphises : A Discussion of his Name, *Numismatic Digest* 25-26 (2001-2002), pp. 43-50, on p. 46.

2 Nicholas Sims-Williams and Joe Cribb, A New Bactrian Inscription of Kanishka the Great, *Silk Road Art and Archaeology* 4 (1995-1996), The Institute of Silk Road Studies, Kamakura, pp. 75-142, figure 11, coin c.

Cribb has read the Kharoshṭhī legend as *Vemasa*, and this has been accepted by Mitchiner.[1]

Class III consists of copper coins, which circulated in the foothill regions of Swat, Hazara, and Kashmir. These coins have the figure of a humped bull standing to the right and a corrupt Greek legend on the obverse, and a two-humped Bactrian camel standing to the right and a Kharoshṭhī legend on the reverse. These coins are in two sizes : the small-sized ones weigh, on an average, 60 grains, and the large-sized ones weigh, on an average, 165 grains.[2] The Greek legend on the obverse of these coins is not fully legible. But on one coin bearing Greek characters on both the sides,[3] Cribb reads *Ooemo Takta*. However, B N Mukherjee[4] is of the view that what has been read as a *tau* by Cribb is actually 'an ill-formed Doric *san* with its semicircle at the top not fully closed', with a trace of an *omikron* after it. On this basis, he reads this part of the coin legend as *Ooemo Taksho*. Cribb

---

1 Michael Mitchiner, The Kushan King, Vima Takshuma, Son of Kujula Kadphises : A Discussion of his Name, *Numismatic Digest* 25-26 (2001-2002), pp. 43-50, on p. 46.

2 Nicholas Sims-Williams and Joe Cribb, A New Bactrian Inscription of Kanishka the Great, *Silk Road Art and Archaeology* 4 (1995-1996), The Institute of Silk Road Studies, Kamakura, pp. 75-142, on pp. 115-118; R C Senior, *Indo-Scythian Coins and History* 2, (London, 2001), p. 221.

3 Nicholas Sims-Williams and Joe Cribb, A New Bactrian Inscription of Kanishka the Great, *Silk Road Art and Archaeology* 4 (1995-1996), The Institute of Silk Road Studies, Kamakura, pp. 75-142, p. 142, figure 15, coin f.

4 B N Mukherjee, The Great Kushāṇa Testament, *Indian Museum Bulletin* 30 (1995), pl. IV, no. 2 (a); B N Mukherjee, Vima Taktu, An Alleged Kushana King, *Numismatic Digest* 21-22 (1997-1998), pp. 5-10, on p. 6.

reads the Kharoshṭhī legend on the reverse of the small-sized coins as *Maharayasa rajàtirajasa devaputrasa Vema Takho*, while Senior[1] reads it as *Maharajasa rajatirajasa devaputrasa Vema Takha-(?)*. But in the reverse legend on one coin, procured by Mitchiner[2] from Mapusa (Goa), the last component of the surname of the issuer is a compound character, of which the top portion is off the flan, while the bottom portion is definitely a *sha* with the *u*-medial quite clear. On this basis, Mitchiner reconstructs the Kharoshṭhī legend on the small-sized coins as *Maharajasa rajatirajasa devaputrasa Vema Takshuma*. According to Cribb,[3] the large-sized coins generally bear, on the reverse, the Kharoshṭhī legend *Maharayasa rayatirayasa devaputrasa Vema Tak[ta] maha*. But there is debate regarding the reading of the last component of the surname of V'ima. This component is a compound character, which has been read as *Taktu* by Senior,[4]

1 R C Senior, *Indo-Scythian Coins and History* 2, (London, 2001), p. 221.

2 Michael Mitchiner, The Kushan King, Vima Takshuma, Son of Kujula Kadphises : A Discussion of his Name, *Numismatic Digest* 25-26 (2001-2002), pp. 43-50, on pp. 47, 48-49 and figures.

3 Nicholas Sims-Williams and Joe Cribb, A New Bactrian Inscription of Kanishka the Great, *Silk Road Art and Archaeology* 4 (1995-1996), The Institute of Silk Road Studies, Kamakura, pp. 75-142, on p. 116, and figure 14, coin a (on p. 141), figure 13, coins b and c (on p. 140); see Michael Mitchiner, The Kushan King, Vima Takshuma, Son of Kujula Kadphises : A Discussion of his Name, *Numismatic Digest* 25-26 (2001-2002), pp. 43-50, on pp. 46-47.

4 R C Senior, *Indo-Scythian Coins and History* 2, (London, 2001), p. 221.

and *Takshuma* by B N Mukherjee.[1] Mitchiner[2] puts forth some arguments in support of Mukherjee's reading. He says that the Kharoshṭhī character *ta* should project only to the left side of the vertical stroke, but a careful observation of the compound character shows there is 'an arcuate, umbrella-like, cross-stroke' passing completely across the vertical stroke. This indicates that this part of the compound character is to be read as *sha*. Also, the *u*-medial is clear in the character, thus indicating that the compound character should be read as *kshu*. On this basis, Mitchiner suggests that what has been read as *Tak[ta] maha* on these large-sized coins, should better be read as *Takshumasa*. According to Mitchiner,[3] one coin has a slightly longer Kharoshṭhī legend, which ends in *Vema Takshumahatasa*;[4] he believes that *Takshumahatasa* is to be understood as the contraction of *Takshuma mahatasa*, with the character *ma* not duplicated. On this basis, he reads the longer legend as *Maharayasa rayatirayasa devaputrasa Vema Takshumahatasa* (= *Vema Takshuma mahatasa*). B N Mukherjee,[5] too, is in the favour of reading the surname of

1 B N Mukherjee, Vima Taktu, An Alleged Kushana King, *Numismatic Digest* 21-22 (1997-1998), pp. 5-10, on pp. 6-7.

2 Michael Mitchiner, The Kushan King, Vima Takshuma, Son of Kujula Kadphises : A Discussion of his Name, *Numismatic Digest* 25-26 (2001-2002), pp. 43-50, on p. 47.

3 Michael Mitchiner, The Kushan King, Vima Takshuma, Son of Kujula Kadphises : A Discussion of his Name, *Numismatic Digest* 25-26 (2001-2002), pp. 43-50, on p. 47.

4 Nicholas Sims-Williams and Joe Cribb, A New Bactrian Inscription of Kanishka the Great, *Silk Road Art and Archaeology* 4 (1995-1996), The Institute of Silk Road Studies, Kamakura, pp. 75-142, on p. 141, figure 14, coin a.

5 B N Mukherjee, Vima Taktu, An Alleged Kushana King, *Numismatic Digest* 21-22 (1997-1998), pp. 5-10, on pp. 6-7.

the issuer as *Takshuma* in the Kharoshṭhī legend on several of these coins.[1] He feels that on the coin with the longer legend,[2] the compound Kharoshṭhī character *kshu* is written horizontally instead of vertically, 'probably due to want of space', but, reading this legend from the outside, he deciphers it as *Takshumasa sishyatrapasa Ya'etiya maharayasa*, which he interprets as '[the coin] of Takshuma, the terror to the ruled, the great king belonging to the Ya'eti'; he identifies Ya'eti as either the Yueh-chihs,[3] or the Iatioi of Ptolemy.[4] However, a careful observation of the coin legend seems to favour the reading proposed by Mitchiner.

Lüders,[5] while translating the Mat inscription, separated Takshuma from V[e]ma, and regarded the donor, Humashpala, as 'the *bakanapati* of Takṣuma (?)', perhaps because Takshuma, compounded with Shāhi V[e]ma, is rendered in the genitive singular case ending (*Takshumasya*), while the titles at the beginning of the record are rendered in the nominative singular. He was, however, 'ready to give up' the joining of *Takshumasya* to *bakanapati* 'if anything

---

1 Nicholas Sims-Williams and Joe Cribb, A New Bactrian Inscription of Kanishka the Great, *Silk Road Art and Archaeology* 4 (1995-1996), The Institute of Silk Road Studies, Kamakura, pp. 75-142, on p. 140, figure 13, coin b; 141, figure 14, coin c; etc.

2 Nicholas Sims-Williams and Joe Cribb, A New Bactrian Inscription of Kanishka the Great, *Silk Road Art and Archaeology* 4 (1995-1996), The Institute of Silk Road Studies, Kamakura, pp. 75-142, on p. 141, figure 14, coin c.

3 B N Mukherjee, Yüeh-chih = Ya'eti, *The Asiatic Society, Monthly Bulletin*, March 1998, pp. 5-6.

4 B N Mukherjee, Vima Taktu, An Alleged Kushana King, *Numismatic Digest* 21-22 (1997-1998), pp. 5-10, on p. 7.

5 Heinrich Lüders, *Mathura Inscriptions*, edited by K L Janert, (Gottingen, 1961), p. 135.

more plausible should be suggested'.[1] B N Mukherjee[2] earlier regarded *Takshuma* as standing for "the appellation of the place of the 'inhabitance or activities' of the (donor) *bakanapati*" or for 'the personal name of the immediate superior official of the *bakanapati*', or for 'a word of unknown meaning'. Konow,[3] and, perhaps, following him, Roman Ghirshman[4] associate Takshuma with V[e]ma, but hold that V[e]ma Takshuma was a Kushāṇa noble, who succeeded V'ima Kadphises, and ruled before Kanishka I. K P Jayaswal[5] is of the view that *Takshama* is an Iranian word meaning 'the brave one'. Thus, he, too, regards *Takshama* as an epithet, and is supported by Konow.[6] Rosenfeld[7] takes V[e]ma as the personal name of the king, and *Takshuma* as his 'descriptive epithet'. Gritli von Mitterwallner[8] also compounds *Takshuma* in the inscription with *Shāhi V[e] ma*, reading it together as *Shāhi V[e]ma Takshuma*. In

---

1 Heinrich Lüders, *Mathura Inscriptions*, edited by K L Janert, (Gottingen, 1961), p. 137.

2 B N Mukherjee, *The Kushāṇa Genealogy*, (Calcutta, 1967), p. 59.

3 Sten Konow, Kalawan Copper-plate Inscription of the Year 134, *Journal of the Royal Asiatic Society of Great Britain and Ireland* (1932), pp. 949-965, on p. 963.

4 Roman Ghirshman, *Begram, Mémoires de la Délégation Archéologique Française en Afghanistan* 13, (Cairo, 1948), p. 140.

5 K P Jayaswal, The Statue of Wema Kadphises and Kushan Chronology, *Journal of the Bihar and Orissa Research Society* 6 (1920), pp. 12-22, on p. 15.

6 Sten Konow, Notes on Indo-Scythian Chronology, *Journal of Indian History* 12 (1933), pp. 1-46, on p. 36.

7 J M Rosenfeld, *The Dynastic Arts of the Kushans*, (Indian edition, New Delhi, 1993), p. 144.

8 Gritli von Mitterwallner, *Kuṣāṇa Coins and Kuṣāṇa Sculptures from Mathurā*, (Mathura, 1986), pp. 58, 59-60.

the context of the Dasht-i-Nawur inscriptions, Humbach[1] takes *Takshuma* as an epithet (‘*beiname*’) of V’ima, and B N Mukherjee,[2] who reads it as *Takshomo*, too, interprets it as ‘an epithet or title of *Ooemo*’. Recently, he argues that Takshuma in the coin legends should also be taken as an epithet of V’ima, on the ground that on one coin,[3] the extant portion of the Kharoshṭhī legend can be deciphered as *...sa Vema mahara[jasa]*;[4] according to him, the very fact, that on some coins, *Takshuma* follows Vema, just as on this coin *maharaja* follows Vema, proves that Vema was the personal name, and *Takshuma* was the epithet associated with it.

Before the discovery of the Rabatak inscription, most of the scholars favoured the identification of *V[e]ma Takshuma* of the Mat inscription and *Ooemo Tak[shomo]* of the Dasht-i-Nawur inscription, as V’ima Kadphises.[5]

---

1 G Djelani Davary and Helmut Humbach, *Die Baktrische Inschrift IDN 1 von Dasht-e Nāwūr (Afghanistan), Akademie der Wissenschaften und der Literatur, Abhandlungen der Geistes- und Sozialwissenschaftlichen Klasse*, Jahrgang 1976, Nr. 1 (Wiesbaden), (1976), pp. 3-21, on p. 6.

2 B N Mukherjee, *Mathura and its Society—The Śaka-Pahlava Phase*, (Calcutta, 1981), pp. 44, 45.

3 Nicholas Sims-Williams and Joe Cribb, A New Bactrian Inscription of Kanishka the Great, *Silk Road Art and Archaeology* 4 (1995-1996), The Institute of Silk Road Studies, Kamakura, pp. 75-142, on p. 142, figure 14, coin b.

4 B N Mukherjee, Vima Taktu, An Alleged Kushana King, *Numismatic Digest* 21-22 (1997-1998), pp. 5-10, on p. 9 and n. 20, and figure 5.

5 J M Rosenfeld, *The Dynastic Arts of the Kushans*, (Indian edition, New Delhi, 1993), pp. 17ff, on 19; G Djelani Davary and Helmut Humbach, *Die Baktrische Inschrift IDN 1 von Dasht-e Nāwūr (Afghanistan), Akademie der Wissenschaften und der Literatur, Abhandlungen der Geistes- und Sozialwissenschaftlichen Klasse*, Jahrgang 1976, Nr. 1 (Wiesbaden), (1976), pp. 3-21, on pp. 10, 20 and

However, the Rabatak inscription shows that *Ooemo Takzoo* (V'ima Takshuma) was the son of Kujula Kadphises, while V'ima Kadphises was the grandson of Kujula Kadphises. This seems to clearly establish the separate identity of V'ima Takshuma and V'ima Kadphises. But recently, B N Mukherjee[1] has expressed the view that, in line 13 of the Rabatak inscription,[2] what has been read as *Ooemo Taktoo* by Sims-Williams,[3] and as *Ooemo Takzoo* by Mitchiner (above), should properly be read as *Sa[dd]ashkano*,[4] which he regards as the name of the son of Kujula Kadphises and the grandfather of Kanishka I.[5] He says that nearly the same name appears as Sadashkaṇa in a gold plaque inscription of Seṇavarma, the king of Oḍi,[6] and that *Sa[dd]ashkano*, the

n 31; B N Mukherjee, *Mathura and its Society—The Śaka-Pahlava Phase*, (Calcutta, 1981), pp. 44, 45; Gritli von Mitterwallner, *Kuṣāṇa Coins and Kuṣāṇa Sculptures from Mathurā*, (Mathura, 1986), pp. 53ff; etc.

1 B N Mukherjee, Vima Taktu, An Alleged Kushana King, *Numismatic Digest* 21-22 (1997-1998), pp. 5-10, on p. 9.

2 Nicholas Sims-Williams and Joe Cribb, A New Bactrian Inscription of Kanishka the Great, *Silk Road Art and Archaeology* 4 (1995-1996), The Institute of Silk Road Studies, Kamakura, pp. 75-142, on p. 135, figure 6.

3 Nicholas Sims-Williams and Joe Cribb, A New Bactrian Inscription of Kanishka the Great, *Silk Road Art and Archaeology* 4 (1995-1996), The Institute of Silk Road Studies, Kamakura, pp. 75-142, on p. 80.

4 B N Mukherjee, The Great Kushāṇa Testament, *Indian Museum Bulletin* 30 (1995), pp. 10, 13.

5 B N Mukherjee, The Great Kushāṇa Testament, *Indian Museum Bulletin* 30 (1995), pp. 15, 17; B N Mukherjee, Vima Taktu, An Alleged Kushana King, *Numismatic Digest* 21-22 (1997-1998), pp. 5-10, on p. 9.

6 H W Bailey, A Kharoṣṭrī Inscription of Seṇavarma, King of Oḍi, *Journal of the Royal Asiatic Society of Great Britain and Ireland*

son of Kujula Kadphises, of the Rabatak inscription should be taken as identical with Sadashkaṇa, the son of Kujula Kadphises, of the Seṇavarma inscription.[1] He, thus, feels that V'ima Taktu or V'ima Takshuma is not mentioned in the Rabatak inscription as the son of Kujula Kadphises. As seen above, he takes *Takshuma* as an epithet, which he associates with V'ima. According to him, there was only one Kushāṇa ruler named V'ima, who had *Kadphises* and *Takshuma* as his titles or epithets.[2]

However, if V'ima Takshuma was identical with V'ima Kadphises, it is hard to explain away the non-occurrence of the two epithets, *Kadphises* and *Takshuma*, together with each other, in any inscription or coin legend, especially when we see a number of epithets being used for the king named Vema in the Mat inscription and in the legend on the coins of Class III (above). As noticed earlier, V'ima Kadphises issued coins in gold, but there are no gold coins either in the anonymous series which has been ascribed to V'ima Takshuma (above) or in the series of coins bearing the whole or part (*Vi*, *Vema*) of the name of V'ima Takshuma (above). Besides, the reading *Sa[dd]ashkano* in line 13 of the Rabatak inscription, as suggested by Mukherjee, is not without difficulty, and has not been taken very seriously by

---

(1980), pp. 21-29, and plate; Richard Salomon, The Inscription of Senavarma, King of Oḍi, *Indo-Iranian Journal* 29 (1986), pp. 261-293.

1 B N Mukherjee, The Great Kushāṇa Testament, *Indian Museum Bulletin* 30 (1995), pp. 10-11; B N Mukherjee, Vima Taktu, An Alleged Kushana King, *Numismatic Digest* 21-22 (1997-1998), pp. 5-10, on pp. 9-10.

2 B N Mukherjee, Vima Taktu, An Alleged Kushana King, *Numismatic Digest* 21-22 (1997-1998), pp. 5-10, on p. 10.

later writers on the subject : Mitchiner[1] does not even refer to it. In the gold plaquc inscription of Seṇavarma, *V'ima* is not mentioned as the first part of the name of Sadashkaṇa. Could Sadashkaṇa of that inscription have been another son of Kujula Kadphises, who was supposed to succeed his father (the use of the title *devaputra* for him in the inscription is worthy of notice here), but death intervened, and V'ima Takshuma attained to kingship after the death of Kujula Kadphises ? We have seen above, that the name of the grandfather of Kanishka I in the Rabatak inscription seems to be divided into two parts, the first of which is restored by most of the scholars as *Ooemo*, while the second part is read variously as *Taktoo*, *Takkashama* or *Takzoo* by them. Thus, the consensus of opinion seems to be in favour of the reading the name of the grandfather of Kanishka I as *Ooemo Taktoo* or *Ooemo Takzoo*. The second component of the ruler's name definitely ends in double *omikron*, and is followed by the title *shao*.[2] This seems to rule out the reading *Sa[dd] ashkano* proposed by Mukherjee. In that case, the Rabatak inscription makes it amply clear that *Ooemo Takzoo* (V'ima Takshuma) was the grandfather of Kanishka I, while *Ooemo Kadphiso* (V'ima Kadphises) was the father of Kanishka I. Therefore, they appear to be two different persons, and the alleged identification of V'ima Takshuma with V'ima Kadphises does not hold ground. V'ima Takshuma, the son

---

1 Michael Mitchiner, The Kushan King, Vima Takshuma, Son of Kujula Kadphises : A Discussion of his Name, *Numismatic Digest* 25-26 (2001-2002), pp. 43-50.

2 Michael Mitchiner, The Kushan King, Vima Takshuma, Son of Kujula Kadphises : A Discussion of his Name, *Numismatic Digest* 25-26 (2001-2002), pp. 43-50, on p. 44.

of Kujula Kadphises, was the father of V'ima Kadphises, and intervened between Kujula Kadphises and V'ima Kadphises.

The vast number of the coins of V'ima Takshuma, and the extensive area from which they are reported, 'testify to a long and powerful reign'.[1] But a very long *independent* reign for V'ima Takshuma is apparently precluded by the fact that his father, Kujula Kadphises, is known from the *Hou Han-shu* (118. 9a) to have ruled till (at least) the age of 80.[2] There is a suggestion that V'ima Takshuma served as the governor of his father in the northern provinces of the Kushāṇa empire for a long time before his accession to the throne, which is hardly surprising in view of the above. V'ima Takshuma, during this period, very probably had his seat at Balkh or Bactria. In the northern provinces of Bactria and Sogdia, the Kushāṇas seem to have had a tradition of issuing coins bearing 'non-personal inscriptions', that is the coin legends mentioned the title(s) of the issuer, and not his personal name.[3] Following this tradition, V'ima Takshuma issued the anonymous coinage with the legend *Basileos basileon soter megas*, while he served his father as governor in the northern provinces. MacDowall[4] observes that the issuer of

1 J M Rosenfeld, *The Dynastic Arts of the Kushans*, (Indian edition, New Delhi, 1993), p. 18; *cf* Alexander Cunningham, Coins of the Śakas, *Numismatic Chronicle* (3rd series) 10 (1890), pp. 103-172, on p. 115.

2 A K Narain, *The Indo-Greeks*, (Oxford, 1957), p. 131; J M Rosenfeld, *The Dynastic Arts of the Kushans*, (Indian edition, New Delhi, 1993), p. 11.

3 Michael Mitchiner, The Kushan King, Vima Takshuma, Son of Kujula Kadphises : A Discussion of his Name, *Numismatic Digest* 25-26 (2001-2002), pp. 43-50, on p. 43.

4 D W MacDowall, Soter Megas, The King of Kings, The Kushāṇa, *Journal of the Numismatic Society of India* 30 (1968), pp. 28-48, on p. 48.

the coins with anonymous series, 'being the founder of a new empire and a new dynasty' (above), was to be known by his grandiloquent titles *Basileos basileon soter megas* only, just as the first Roman emperor Octavian ceased using his personal name, and came to be known by the titles *Cæsar Augustus Imperator*, after the Battle of Actium. But the explanation of Mitchiner for the 'non-personal inscriptions' on these coins is more acceptable than that of MacDowall, because the issuer of this series (V'ima Takshuma) was the son and successor of Kujula Kadphises as per the evidence of the Rabatak inscription (above), and not 'the founder of a new empire and a new dynasty' as MacDowall believed. Perhaps, V'ima Takshuma's being a governor under Kujula Kadphises would explain the fact, observed by M E Masson,[1] that the 'palaeography on coins of *Soter Megas* (that is, V'ima Takshuma) shows the same wide range of letter forms that we find on the various coinages of Kujula Kadphises'. According to the *Hou Han-shu* (118. 9a), Kujula Kadphises was succeeded by his son, Yen-kao-chen, who conquered India and appointed military commanders as governors there.[2] This Yen-kao-chen should now be identified with V'ima Takshuma. He would have immediately succeeded his father, and there could not possibly have been scope for any chronological break between Kujula Kadphises and V'ima Takshuma, in which to place the dynasty of Gondopharnes

1 *vide* D W MacDowall, Soter Megas, The King of Kings, The Kushāṇa, *Journal of the Numismatic Society of India* 30 (1968), pp. 28-48, on p. 38.

2 J M Rosenfeld, *The Dynastic Arts of the Kushans*, (Indian edition, New Delhi, 1993), p. 17.

as proposed by MacDowall.[1] V'ima Takshuma might have carried on the tradition of issuing coins with 'non-personal inscriptions' even after ascending the throne.[2] As the issuer of the anonymous coinage, V'ima Takshuma has been given the credit for several innovations in the Kushāṇa coinage. The coinage of Kujula Kadphises was local in character, that is he 'almost always follows the pattern of the denominations that he found in each of his provinces'. V'ima Takshuma initially seems to have had followed a similar pattern, but later on, he inaugurated a 'general coinage' (above) for circulation throughout his empire, and this system of uniform coinage was adopted and elaborated upon by his son, V'ima Kadphises.[3] The coinage of Kujula Kadphises does not, in general, have his personal symbol or *tamga*, although some of his coins do have a peculiar symbol made of a circle and three prongs. V'ima Takshuma started the practice of placing his personal symbol invariably on all his coins, and this practice—the origin of which has been traced back to the Gondopharnes symbol—was followed by his successors like V'ima Kadphises, Kanishka I, and others.[4] V'ima Takshuma could be said to have had a 'long' reign, if this is taken to

1 D W MacDowall, Soter Megas, The King of Kings, The Kushāṇa, *Journal of the Numismatic Society of India* 30 (1968), pp. 28-48, on pp. 43ff.

2 Michael Mitchiner, The Kushan King, Vima Takshuma, Son of Kujula Kadphises : A Discussion of his Name, *Numismatic Digest* 25-26 (2001-2002), pp. 43-50, on p. 43.

3 D W MacDowall, Soter Megas, The King of Kings, The Kushāṇa, *Journal of the Numismatic Society of India* 30 (1968), pp. 28-48, on pp. 39, 41.

4 D W MacDowall, Soter Megas, The King of Kings, The Kushāṇa, *Journal of the Numismatic Society of India* 30 (1968), pp. 28-48, on p. 42.

include the period he served as the governor of his father in the northern provinces of the Kushāṇa empire, together with his independent rule.

It has been mentioned above, that the *Soter Megas* coins are reported from Kandahar and the Kabul valley, and from the region extending from Mathura to Peshawar and into Russian Turkestan; some coins are reported from as far east as Varanasi and Ghazipur in eastern Uttar Pradesh. The *provenance* of these coins gives as an idea of the extensive Kushāṇa dominions under V'ima Takshuma. The fact that some of the Arachosian type of coins of Pakores are found restruck on the coins of *Soter Megas* (= V'ima Takshuma) seems to testify to the hold of that Kushāṇa ruler over the Arachosia region.[1] The discovery of the coins of *Soter Megas* (= V'ima Takshuma) during the excavations at Shaikhan Dheri in the Charsadda area of Pakistan, indicates his hold over the Pushkalāvatī region.[2]

There are two more inscriptions, which might have been associated with V'ima Takshuma, though this is by no means certain. A fragmentary inscribed *Śivaliṅgaṁ* has been found from Reh in the Fatehpur district of Uttar Pradesh.[3] The name of the ruler mentioned in the inscription is not clear, although G R Sharma has tried to read it as Minandra

1 B N Mukherjee, *An Agrippan Source—A Study in Indo-Parthian History*, (Calcutta, 1969), pp. 217, 242-243.

2 A H Dani, Shaikhan Dheri Excavation, 1963 and 1964 Seasons, *Ancient Pakistan* 3, (1965-1966), p. 38, and chart no. 2; B N Mukherjee, *An Agrippan Source—A Study in Indo-Parthian History*, (Calcutta, 1969), p. 230, n. 7.

3 P L Gupta, *Prāchīna Bhārata ke Pramukha Abhilekha*, (Hindi, Varanasi, 1996), pp. 139ff.

(= Menander).[1] However, the ruler has been ascribed the titles of *maharaja rajatiraja mahaṁta tratara dhammika.* As pointed out by P L Gupta, the use of *maharaja rajatiraja* for a ruler is not known prior to the Indo-Greeks, and Sharma's ascription of the inscription to Menander seems untenable. The first four titles in the inscription are the Prakrit rendering of the Greek *Basileos basileon soter megas*. P L Gupta proposes to identify the ruler mentioned in the Reh inscription with V'ima Kadphises,[2] who uses the Greek titles *basileos basileon soter megas* on the obverse of some of his copper coins.[3] However, it may be mentioned here that *basileos basileon* has been rendered into Prakrit as *maharaja rajatiraja*, and *soter* as *tratara*, in the reverse inscription on these coins, but there is no Prakrit equivalent of the Greek *megas* in the reverse legend. It is likely, though not certain, that the Reh inscription refers to *Soter Megas* (= V'ima Takshuma), whose coins bear these Greek titles as legend on the obverse, and the Prakrit rendering of these Greek titles as legend on the reverse, without mentioning the name of the king. If this be accepted, it would seem to show that V'ima Takshuma held sway over eastern Uttar Pradesh, which is corroborated by the finds of his coins from Varanasi and Ghazipur (above).

---

1 G R Sharma, *The Reh Inscription of Menander and the Indo-Greek Invasion of the Gaṅgā Valley*, Studies in History, Culture and Archaeology 1, Allahabad, 1980.

2 P L Gupta, *Prāchīna Bhārata ke Pramukha Abhilekha*, (Hindi, Varanasi, 1996), p. 140.

3 Percy Gardner, *Catalogue of the Coins of the Greek and Scythic Kings of Bactria and India, In the British Museum, London*, (reprint, New Delhi, 1971), p. 126, pl. XXV. 12.

Then, there is a two line inscription found from the village of Khalatse, about 52 miles from Leh in Ladakh, Jammu and Kashmir.[1] Rapson, in a letter addressed to A H Francke, dated 23.09.1910, reported that, from the photograph of the inscription supplied to him, he could read, though with some doubt, the date 187 in line 1 of the inscription. In line 2, he could read the word *maharajasa*, followed by a name, which, perhaps, began with the character *a*.[2] Sten Konow also tried to read the inscription from the same photograph sent to Rapson, and from the 'imperfect' plate published by Francke.[3] He read the name, ending with the genitive termination, as *Uvimakavthisasa*, and identified the ruler as V'ima Kadphises.[4] D C Sircar, using the photograph published by Sten Konow in his *Corpus*,[5] read the name of the ruler in the inscription as *Uvimikastu(vṭu ?)sa*.[6] However, one can get an idea of the difficulty in reading the name of the ruler in the inscription from the statement of Sircar, that the

---

1 Sten Konow, *Corpus Inscriptionum Indicarum* 2(1), Kharoshṭhī Inscriptions with the Exceptions of those of Aśoka, (Calcutta, 1929), pp.79-81.

2 *vide* Sten Konow, *Corpus Inscriptionum Indicarum* 2(1), Kharoshṭhī Inscriptions with the Exceptions of those of Aśoka, (Calcutta, 1929), p. 79.

3 Sten Konow, *Corpus Inscriptionum Indicarum* 2(1), Kharoshṭhī Inscriptions with the Exceptions of those of Aśoka, (Calcutta, 1929), p. 79.

4 Sten Konow, *Corpus Inscriptionum Indicarum* 2(1), Kharoshṭhī Inscriptions with the Exceptions of those of Aśoka, (Calcutta, 1929), p. 80.

5 Sten Konow, *Corpus Inscriptionum Indicarum* 2(1), Kharoshṭhī Inscriptions with the Exceptions of those of Aśoka, (Calcutta, 1929), pl. XV. 2.

6 D C Sircar, *Select Inscriptions* 1 (Delhi, 1986), p. 134.

second character of the name may also be read as *cha*, *ri*, or *ti*, and the third character, as *da* or *de*.[1] The fourth character has been read by both Sten Konow and D C Sircar as *ka*. But Sten Konow mentions that the third character is 'almost running' into the fourth character. There is also a flaw in the stone at this place.[2] D C Sircar further says that the reading of the fifth character is doubtful.[3] Sten Konow also regards it as 'the most difficult akshara of the whole inscription'.[4] Sten Konow tentatively proposes to read it as *vthi*, and D C Sircar, as *stu* or *vṭu*. D C Sircar has frankly admitted that the identity of the ruler mentioned in this inscription is, by no means, certain. Is it possible that this ruler is V'ima Takshuma, and not V'ima Kadphises, as suggested by Sten Konow ? The era to which the year 187 of the Khalatse inscription should be referred is difficult to determine.

If the Khalatse inscription may be ascribed to V'ima Takshuma (above), it would vouch for his hold over the Ladakh-Kashmir region. Again, if P L Gupta's ascription of the Reh inscription to *Soter Megas* (who should be identified with V'ima Takshuma as seen above, and not with V'ima Kadphises as proposed by P L Gupta) be accepted (above), it would show that V'ima Takshuma also ruled over parts of eastern Uttar Pradesh, from where the *Soter Megas* coins, too, are reported. This would seem to indicate that, during the

1 *Select Inscriptions* 1 (Delhi, 1986), p. 134, n. 2.

2 Sten Konow, *Corpus Inscriptionum Indicarum* 2(1), Kharoshṭhī Inscriptions with the Exceptions of those of Aśoka, (Calcutta, 1929), p. 80.

3 D C Sircar, *Select Inscriptions* 1 (Delhi, 1986), p. 134.

4 Sten Konow, *Corpus Inscriptionum Indicarum* 2(1), Kharoshṭhī Inscriptions with the Exceptions of those of Aśoka, (Calcutta, 1929), p. 80.

reign of V'ima Takshuma, the Kushāṇa dominions extended from eastern Uttar Pradesh in the east to the Kabul valley in the west, and into Russian Turkestan.

Incidentally, the *Hou Han-shu* refers to the son and successor of Kujula Kadphises as Yen-kao-chen. Now that we know, from epigraphic and numismatic sources, that the Graeco-Bactrian form of the name of the son and successor of Kujula Kadphises was *Ooemo Takzoo/Ooemo Tak[shomo]*, and the Kharoshṭhī-Brāhmī form was *V'ima Takshuma/ V'ima Tākshuma*, it becomes difficult to understand their correlation with Yen-kao-chen. It has been suggested that the Chinese chronicler was either using an alternative form of the name of the son and successor of Kujula Kadphises, or *Yen-kao-chen* was the title of that ruler.[1]

It may, *en passant*, be mentioned here that the numismatic and epigraphic evidence to indicate that V'ima Takshuma ruled over parts of eastern Uttar Pradesh (above), would, perhaps, explain as to how Kanishka I was able to issue inscriptions in that region in the early years of his reign—his Kosam inscription from the Allahabad district has been ascribed variously to his second or third year,[2] and his Sarnath inscription is dated in his third year.[3] For years, scholars have found it difficult to explain as to how Kanishka I, if he succeeded V'ima Kadphises in the northwestern

1 Nicholas Sims-Williams and Joe Cribb, A New Bactrian Inscription of Kanishka the Great, *Silk Road Art and Archaeology* 4 (1995-1996), The Institute of Silk Road Studies, Kamakura, pp. 75-142, on pp. 75-142; *cf* Michael Mitchiner, The Kushan King, Vima Takshuma, Son of Kujula Kadphises : A Discussion of his Name, *Numismatic Digest* 25-26 (2001-2002), pp. 43-50, on p. 48.

2 D C Sircar, *Select Inscriptions* 1 (Delhi, 1986), pp. 135-136, and p. 136, n. 2.

3 D C Sircar, *Select Inscriptions* 1 (Delhi, 1986), pp. 136-137.

India, could issue inscriptions in eastern Uttar Pradesh in the early years of his reign. Some, like J F Fleet,[1] A von Staël Holstein[2] and Sten Konow,[3] have suggested that Kanishka I was not a scion of the family of the Ta Yueh-chih, to which the Kadphises group of kings belonged. On the contrary, the last two scholars have sought to associate Kanishka I with the Hsiao Yueh-chih, on the basis of the doubtful evidence of the *Ma-ming-p'u-sa-chuan*, the biography of Aśvaghosha, and of Kumārajīva's gloss of the name *Tou-ch'u-lo* as 'Little Yue-chih' in the Chinese translation of the *Mahāprajñā-pāramitā(sūtra)śāstra.*[4] Other scholars, like D C Sircar[5] and Sudhakar Chattopadhyaya,[6] suggest that Kanishka I rose to power in eastern Uttar Pradesh, where he was initially serving as a governor of V'ima Kadphises and from where his early inscriptions have been found, and that, after asserting his independence, he extended his sway towards the west. But B N Mukherjee has shown that the *Hou*

---

1 J F Fleet, A Hitherto Unrecognised Kushāṇ King, *Journal of the Royal Asiatic Society of Great Britain and Ireland*, 1903, pp. 325-334, on p. 334.

2 *vide* B N Mukherjee, *The Kushāṇa Genealogy* (Calcutta, 1967), p. 48.

3 Sten Konow, *Corpus Inscriptionum Indicarum* 2(1), Kharoshṭhī Inscriptions with the Exceptions of those of Aśoka, (Calcutta, 1929), p. lxxvi.

4 See B N Mukherjee, *The Kushāṇa Genealogy* (Calcutta, 1967), pp. 48-49.

5 D C Sircar, The Kushāṇas. Chapter IX in R C Majumdar, A D Pusalker, and A K Majumdar (ed), *The Age of Imperial Unity* (History and Culture of the Indian People 2, Bombay, 1980), pp. 136-153, on p. 141.

6 Sudhakar Chattopadhyaya, *Early History of North India* (Delhi, 1976), p. 99.

Han-shu and the *San-kuo* of Ch'en Shou seem to associate Kanishka I with the Ta Yueh-chih.[1] And now we also have the Rabatak inscription, which clearly associates Kanishka I with the Kadphises group of kings, and refers to him as the son of V'ima Kadphises, grandson of V'ima Takshuma, and great grandson of Kujula Kadphises. Kushāṇa dominions had extended as far east as eastern Uttar Pradesh as early as the time of V'ima Takshuma, and, as such, there is no problem in understanding as to how Kanishka I could have issued inscriptions dated in the early years of his reign in eastern Uttar Pradesh. He had inherited regions as far east as eastern Uttar Pradesh from his ancestors; the credit for carrying Kushāṇa arms further east, at least as far as Bihar, should be given to Kanishka himself.[2]

Kācha. The coins of the Kācha type (coins no. 20, 21), all in gold, bear, on the obverse, the standing figure of the king, dressed in coat and trousers, and holding a *chakradhvaja* in his left hand, while he is sacrificing at an altar with his right hand. There is the vertical legend, *Kācha*, under the left arm of the king. The circular legend reads *Kācho gāmavajitya divaṁ karmabhiruttamairjayati*. The reverse has a standing goddess (Lakshmī ?), holding a flower in her right hand, and a *cornucopiae* in her left hand. One variety, known from the Bayana hoard, has similar depictions on both the sides of the coin, but there is a *garuḍadhvaja* in front of the king on the obverse, and the goddess on the reverse holds a *pāśa* in

1 Sudhakar Chattopadhyaya, *Early History of North India* (Delhi, 1976), p. 99.

2 Sudhakar Chattopadhyaya, *Early History of North India* (Delhi, 1976), pp. 101ff.

her right hand, in place of the flower.[1] Right from the first discovery of the gold coins of Kācha, his place in Imperial Gupta history has occupied the imagination of historians, mainly because his name does not find mention either in the Imperial Gupta genealogy given in their inscriptions and seals, or in literature.[2]

B S Sitholey was one of the very few scholars, who were not ready to accept Kācha as a scion of the Imperial Gupta dynasty. His main argument in support of his stand was that, had Kācha been an Imperial Gupta ruler, his name, like the names of all the other Imperial Guptas (barring that of Ghaṭotkacha, the father of Chandragupta I), would have had *-gupta* as the name ending. He regards Kācha as some high official in the service of Samudragupta, who occupied the Imperial Gupta throne when his master led military campaign against the rulers of *dakshiṇāpatha*, and who was disposed of when Samudragupta returned to Pāṭaliputra from his successful southern expedition.[3]

---

1 See A S Altekar, *The Coinage of the Gupta Empire*, (Corpus of Indian Coins 4), (Varanasi, 1957), p. 78. The coin-hoards containing his coins come from Jaunpur, Tanda (Faizabad district), Kasarva (Ballia district), Kumarkhan (Ahmadabad district) and Sakori (Damoh district). A S Altekar, *The Coinage of the Gupta Empire*, (Corpus of Indian Coins 4), (Varanasi, 1957), pp. 307ff.

2 The Kaliyugarājavṛittānta of the *Bhavishyottarapurāṇa*, in which his name occurs, is a modern forgery. See R C Majumdar, A Forged Purāṇa Text on the Imperial Guptas, *Indian Historical Quarterly* 20, (1944), pp. 345-350; D C Sircar, *Bhavishyottarapurāṇa* and Early Gupta History, *Journal of the Numismatic Society of India* 6, (1944), pp. 34-36.

3 B S Sitholey, Was Kācha a Gupta Monarch ?, *Journal of the Numismatic Society of India* 12, (1950), pp. 38-40. It may, however, be mentioned here that though A S Altekar regards Kācha as a scion

Buddha Prakash[1] and M J Sharma[2] propose to identify Kācha of the gold coins with the first of the two persons named Kācha mentioned in an Ajanta inscription.[3] The latter scholar is of the view that Kācha was a loyal high officer of Samudragupta, who sided with the rightfully chosen heir of Chandragupta I, in his struggle against the rival claimants to the Imperial Gupta throne. When Samudragupta had consolidated his position, he issued the Kācha type of coins to express his gratitude to Kācha for his support.[4] Sharma further suggests that Kācha might have been a brother of Dattadevī, the queen of Samudragupta.[5]

However, the depiction of the *garuḍadhvaja* on the obverse of Class II of the coins of Kācha, known only for a single specimen in the Bayana hoard,[6] establishes beyond doubt that Kācha belonged to the Imperial Gupta family, which had the *garuḍa* as its royal insignia. But the question,

---

of the Imperial Gupta family, he does not altogether rule out the possibility of his being an upstart, who usurped the Imperial Gupta throne for a short while. A S Altekar, *Coinage of the Gupta Empire*, (Varanasi, 1957), p. 79.

1 Buddha Prakash, *Aspects of Indian History and Civilization*, (Agra, 1965), pp. 80ff.

2 M J Sharma, The Identification of Kācha—A Fresh Study, *Journal of the Epigraphical Society of India* 1, (1974), pp. 75-84.

3 *Archaeological Survey of Western India* 4, p. 129.

4 M J Sharma, The Identification of Kācha—A Fresh Study, *Journal of the Epigraphical Society of India* 1, (1974), pp. 75-84, on p. 79.

5 M J Sharma, The Identification of Kācha—A Fresh Study, *Journal of the Epigraphical Society of India* 1, (1974), pp. 75-84, on p. 83, n. 25.

6 A S Altekar, *Catalogue of the Gupta Gold Coins in the Bayana Hoard*, (Bombay, 1954), p. 62.

which agitated the minds of historians, was : 'Where to place Kācha in Imperial Gupta genealogy ?'

Some scholars propose to identify Kācha of coins with *Mahārāja* Ghaṭotkacha, the second Gupta ruler.[1] But it is often argued that the father of Chandragupta I was a mere *mahārāja*, and he could not have issued gold coins. Sibesh Bhattacharya, too, identifies Kācha as Ghaṭotkacha, the father of Chandragupta I, but suggests that these coins were issued by Samudragupta to commemorate his grandfather.[2] Similar is the view of Joe Cribb.[3]

B Ch Chhabra derives the name Kācha from *-kacha*, the second part of the name of Ghaṭotkacha, and suggests that Kācha was a son of Ghaṭotkacha and a brother of Chandragupta I, and that this Kācha ruled for a short while between Chandragupta I and Samudragupta.[4]

K K Thaplyal, mainly on the basis of the occurrence of the *garuḍadhvaja* on Class II of the Kācha coins, proposes to identify Kācha as a brother, most likely an elder one, of Samudragupta. This son of Chandragupta I, going against the express wishes of his father regarding succession, occupied

---

1 James Prinsep, *Journal of the Asiatic Society of Bengal* 53, p. 2, n. 4, *vide* D R Bhandarkar, Inscriptions of the Early Gupta Kings, *Corpus Inscriptionum Indicarum* 3, (New Delhi, 1981), p. 51, n. 1; F W Thomas, *vide* A S Altekar, *The Coinage of the Gupta Empire*, (Corpus of Indian Coins 4), (Varanasi, 1957), p. 79.

2 Sibesh Bhattacharya, Ghaṭotkacha : the King Kācha of Coins, in B Ch Chhabra, *et al* (ed), *Reappraising Gupta History for S R Goyal*, (New Delhi, 1992), pp. 77-82.

3 Joe Cribb, The Late Kushan Type Gold Coins of Mashra, *Coin Hoards* 7, (1985), pp. 306-307.

4 B Ch Chhabra, *Catalogue of the Gold Coins of the Bayana Hoard, in the National Museum*, (New Delhi, 1986), p. xvii.

the Imperial Gupta throne after Chandragupta I, only to be displaced by Samudragupta after a short while.

R D Banerji was of the opinion that Kācha was an elder brother or some near relation of Samudragupta, who lost his life during the struggle of Chandragupta I against the Kushāṇas, and that Samudragupta, on becoming king, issued coins to commemorate this hero, who had sacrificed his life in the struggle for liberation from foreign (Kushāṇa) rule.[1]

Quite interesting is the view of a number of scholars, like J F Fleet,[2] J Allan,[3] R K Mookerji,[4] H C Raychaudhuri,[5] R G Basak,[6] T P Verma,[7] and, most recently, Ashvini Agrawal,[8] proposed to identify Kācha with Samudragupta, on various grounds. Of particular interest here is the dilemma faced by V A Smith over the issue. This scholar was earlier in favour

---

1 R D Banerji, *The Age of the Imperial Guptas,* (Banaras, 1933), p. 9.

2 J F Fleet, Inscriptions of the Early Gupta Kings and their Successors, *Corpus Inscriptionum Indicarum* 3, (Calcutta, 1888), p. 27, n. 4.

3 John Allan, Catalogue *of the Coins of the Gupta Dynasties, and of Śaśāṅka, the King of Gauḍa, in the British Museum, London*, (London, 1914), Introduction, p. xxxiii.

4 R K Mookerji, *The Gupta Empire*, (Delhi, 1947), p. 17.

5 H C Raychaudhuri, Political *History of Ancient India*, (with a commentary by B N Mukherjee), (Oxford, 2004), p. 533.

6 R G Basak, *The History of North-eastern India*, (Calcutta, 1967), pp. 38-39.

7 T P Verma, Samudragupta : the Founder of the Gupta Dynasty, in B Ch Chhabra *et al* (ed), *Reappraising Gupta History for S R Goyal*, (New Delhi, 1992), pp. 83-110, on pp. 102-104.

8 Ashvini Agrawal, The Place of Kācha in Gupta Genealogy, *Journal of the Numismatic Society of India* 43, (1981), pp. 71-74, on p. 73; also *Rise and Fall of the Imperial Guptas*, (Delhi, 1989), p. 105.

of identifying Kācha with Samudragupta.[1] But four years later, he proposed to regard them as two separate rulers.[2] And, before another ten years had elapsed, he reverted to his earlier stand, and, once again, identified the two.[3]

In the *Āryamañjuśrīmūlakalpa*, it is mentioned that Samudra[-gupta] had a younger brother, named Bhasma.[4] This led K P Jayaswal to suggest that, *kācha* and *bhasma* being synonymous, Kācha of coins should be identified as a younger brother and successor of Samudragupta,[5] a view, which has the support of some other scholars as well.[6]

Quite interesting is the view of Aparna Chattopadhyay, that Kācha was a rival of Samudragupta, and, in order to win his goodwill, Samudragupta issued coins in the name of Kācha, the identity of the issuer being revealed by the legend,

---

1 V A Smith, Catalogue of the Coins of Gupta Dynasty, *Journal of the Royal Asiatic Society of Great Britain and Ireland*, 1889, pp. 74-76.

2 V A Smith, Observations on the Gupta Coinage, *Journal of the Royal Asiatic Society of Great Britain and Ireland*, 1893, pp. 77-148, on p. 95.

3 V A Smith, Revised Chronology of the Early or Imperial Gupta Dynasty, *Indian Antiquary* 31, 1902, pp. 257-266, on p. 259.

4 K P Jayaswal, *An Imperial History of India*, c *700 BC* – c *770 AD*, (reprint, Patna, 1988), text p. 42. Also J Agrawal, cited by Ashvini Agrawal, *Rise and Fall of the Imperial Guptas*, (Delhi, 1989), p. 136; P L Gupta, *The Imperial Guptas* 1, (Varanasi, 1998), pp. 122ff.

5 K P Jayaswal, *An Imperial History of India*, c *700 BC* – c *770 AD*, (reprint, Patna, 1988), pp. 48-49.

6 P L Gupta, *The Imperial Guptas* 1, (Varanasi, 1998), p. 256; S R Goyal, *Imperial Guptas*, (Jodhpur, 2005), pp. 182-183, 186; L P Pandey, *Kāśī Nagari Pracharini Patrika*, Saṁvat 2034, parts 3-4, pp. 53ff.See also, K D Bajpai, *Indian Numismatic Studies*, (New Delhi, 1976), pp. 135-137; Prashant Srivastava, *Aspects of Ancient Indian Numismatics*, (Delhi, 1986), pp. 272-273.

sarvvarāj=ochchhettā, occurring on the reverse of the coins. This Kācha, she feels, might be the same as Bhasma of the *Āryamañjuśrīmūlakalpa.*[1]

D R Bhandarkar was of the view that the name Rāmagupta, in the *Devīchandraguptam* of Viśākhadatta, was a scribal error for Kāchagupta,[2] a view, which was, at one time, accepted by scholars like Altekar.[3] But the mention of *Mahārājādhirāja* Rāmagupta in three epigraphs of the Gupta period from Durjanpur near Vidiśā,[4] and the find of copper coins of the Imperial Gupta period, bearing the name of Rāmagupta, from Vidiśā, Eran, and their neighbourhood,[5] would render Bhandarkar's view untenable.

1 Aparna Chattopadhyay, A Note on the Kācha Problem of Gupta History, *Journal of the Oriental Institute (Baroda)* 22(1-2), (1972), pp. 64-67.

2 D R Bhandarkar, New Light on the Early Gupta History, in *Malaviya Commemoration Volume*, (Varanasi, 1932), pp. 189-211; Inscriptions of the Early Gupta Kings, *Corpus Inscriptionum Indicarum* 3, (New Delhi, 1981), p. 51.

3 A S Altekar, *The Coinage of the Gupta Empire*, (Corpus of Indian Coins 4), (Varanasi, 1957), pp. 84-85.

4 D R Bhandarkar, Inscriptions of the Early Gupta Kings, *Corpus Inscriptionum Indicarum* 3, (New Delhi, 1981), pp. 231-234.

5 A S Altekar, *The Coinage of the Gupta Empire*, (Corpus of Indian Coins 4), (Varanasi, 1957), pp. 162-164.

6

Rarity of royal figures and realistic portraiture on indigenous coins

On at least three occasions, I have commented upon the rarity of busts and of realistic portraiture on early Indian indigenous coins, and speculated on some probable explanations.[1]

It is seen that the obverse of the Indo-Greek coins is usually occupied by the head or bust of the king, and queen/mother also in some instances (coins no. 22-28).[2] This feature seems to have been adopted on Indo-Greek coins from the

---

1 Prashant Srivastava, On the Rarity of Busts and of Realistic Portraiture on Indigenous Indian Coins, *Pañchāla* (Journal of the Pañchāla Research Institute) 10, (1997), pp. 131-134; Prashant Srivastava, *Art Motifs on Ancient Indian Coins*, (New Delhi, 2004), pp. 10-14; Prashant Srivastava, Further Observations on the Rarity of Busts and of Realistic Portraiture on Early Indian Indigenous Coins, in S Z H Jafri and N R Farooqi (ed), *Pluralities of Past—Upper Gangetic Valley through the Millennium*, (New Delhi, 2012), pp. 144-151.

2 Prashant Srivastava, *Aspects of Ancient Indian Numismatics*, (Delhi, 1996), pl. I. 2; pl. II. 2; etc.

coins of the Seleukid kings of Syria.[1] After the Indo-Greeks, this numismatic tradition was continued, after a break, by some Śaka-Pahlava kings, like Orthagnes,[2] Gondopharnes,[3] Pakores,[4] and others. Some Kushāṇa coins also bear the bust of the issuing monarch (coins no. 29-32).[5] The silver coins of the Kshaharāta Kshatrapas (coins no. 33-35), and the Kārddamaka Kshatrapas (coins no. 36-42) of western India invariably bear the bust of the issuer on the obverse,[6] and, perhaps, under the influence of these coins, some indigenous powers, like the Sātavāhanas[7] (coins no. 43-44), the Traikūṭakas (coins no. 49-50), and the Imperial Guptas[8] (coins no. 45-48) also depicted the royal bust on the obverse of their silver coins.

---

1 B N Mukherjee, A Plea for the Study of Art in Coinage, *Journal of the Numismatic Society of India* 43(1), (1981), pp. 1ff, on pp. 4-5.

2 Prashant Srivastava, *Aspects of Ancient Indian Numismatics*, (Delhi, 1996), pl. IV. 2.

3 Percy Gardner, *Catalogue of the Coins of the Greek and Scythic Kings of Bactria and India, in the British Museum, London*, (reprint, New Delhi, 1971), pl. XXII. 11.

4 John H Marshall, *Taxila* 3, (reprint, Delhi, 1975), pl. 241. 201.

5 Percy Gardner, *Catalogue of the Coins of the Greek and Scythic Kings of Bactria and India, in the British Museum, London*, (reprint, New Delhi, 1971), pl. XXV. 5—Kujula Kadphises; *ibid*., pl. XXV. 10—V'ima Kadphises; *ibid*., pl. XXVI. 17—Kanishka I; *ibid*., p. 143, coin no 57—Huvishka.

6 E J Rapson, *Catalogue of the Coins of the Andhra Dynasty, the Western Kṣatrapas, the Traikūṭaka Dynasty, and the "Bodhi" Dynasty, in the British Museum, London*, (reprint, New Delhi, 1975), pls. Xff.

7 Mala Dutta, *A Study of the Sātavāhana Coinage*, (New Delhi, 1990), pl. XVIII. 69.

8 A S Altekar, *The Coinage of the Gupta Empire*, (Corpus of Indian Coins 4), (Varanasi, 1957), pl. XVI. 3-6.

Depiction of merely the head or bust of the king on coins was never very popular among the indigenous powers in ancient India. When the royal bust or head appeared on early Indian indigenous coins (like those of the Sātavāhanas and the Imperial Guptas), it was due, mainly, to foreign influence. Indians usually depicted the full-length figure of the king on their coins, instead of just the bust or head.

Similar is the case with divine and animal figures as well. Heads of deities appear on Greek coins,[1] and, following their example, on Hellenistic coins in Asia, like on the Indo-Greek series.[2] Similarly, heads of animals make their appearance on Greek,[3] Indo-Greek,[4] and Śaka-Pahlava coins.[5] On ancient Indian indigenous coins, deities are represented anthropomorphically, theriomorphically, or symbolically. When depicted anthropo-morphically, the whole figure of the deity is usually represented, not merely the head or bust. Even in sculptural art, depiction of mere head of a deity is not common in ancient India; the most famous example of such a depiction is the three-headed bust of Śiva Maheśvara

---

1 Percy Gardner, *A History of Ancient Coinage (700-300 BC)*, (Oxford, 1918), pl. II. 12—head of Athena.

2 A N Lahiri, *Corpus of Indo-Greek Coins*, (Calcutta, 1965), pl. XXV. 2—head of Athena.

3 Percy Gardner, *A History of Ancient Coinage (700-300 BC)*, (Oxford, 1918), pl. II. 5—head of bull.

4 A N Lahiri, *Corpus of Indo-Greek Coins*, (Calcutta, 1965), pl. XII. 9—head of elephant.

5 R B Whitehead, *Catalogue of the Coins in the Punjab Museum, Lahore* 1, The Indo-Greek Coins, (Oxford, 1914), pl. X. 5—head of elephant.

at Elephanta, datable to the eighth century AD.[1] Mere heads of animals, too, are hard to find on ancient Indian indigenous coins.

What could be the possible reason(s) for this aversion to the depiction of merely the head or bust of the divine and royal figures and head of animals, on the part of the Indian die-cutters ?

One reason could be that when merely the head or bust of a figure is depicted on coins, the beholder has to form a notion of the other limbs and parts of the body of the person or animal depicted. 'But such a conception would be a matter of inference and not of portrayal.' This was quite contrary to the traditional principles of the Indian art of portrayal, which demanded of the artist to draw 'all the limbs of the portrayed object', and to 'leave nothing for inference (*sarvāṅga-dṛiśyakaraṇaṁ chitraṁ ity-abhidhīyate*)'.[2]

Reference to natural form is an essential quality of Indian plastic and pictorial art.[3] In fact, Yaśodhara, the author of the *Jayamaṅgala* commentary on the *Kāmasūtra* of Vātsyāyana, refers to *sādṛiśyaṁ* as one of the six limbs (*shaḍaṅga*) of painting, the principles of which are believed to have been almost equally applicable also on sculpture, carving, etc, thereby showing the importance of *sādṛiśyaṁ* in Indian plastic and pictorial art. P K Agrawala is of the view that the *shaḍaṅga* theory is much older than the time of Yaśodhara (eleventh century AD), and says that certain passages in the *Dūtavākya* of Bhāsa (whom he places not later than the

1 Heinrich Robert Zimmer, *The Art of Indian Asia, its Mythology and Transformations*, (completed and edited by Joseph Campbell), (New York, 1955), pl. 253.

2 S N Dasgupta, *Fundamentals of Indian Art*, (Bombay, 1954), p. 57.

3 *Cf Vishṇudharmottarapurāṇa* III. 42-43; *Śilparatna* IV. 46. 145-146.

second-third centuries AD) and the *Divyāvadāna* of the same period, may be analyzed with reference to the *shaḍaṅga* principles, including *sādṛiśyaṁ.*[1] N R Ray observes that *sādṛiśyaṁ* 'does not mean exact likeness to an object, but it does mean a kind of verisimilitude with or reference to the corresponding object in life and nature so that it receives general consent from the beholder.'[2]

The depiction of the bust or head of king on Indo-Greek coins is very realistic, with the various stages of life—boyhood, youth, and old age, clearly shown on some coins. For instance, Strato I appears, on his various coins,[3] as a young man, a mature person, and as an old man 'with toothless jaws and sunken cheeks'.[4] This feature of Indo-Greek coins, too, is due to Seleukid inspiration. It has been observed that realistic portraiture of the king on coins was due to the fact that the peoples of these regions 'were accustomed to the rule of individuals with absolute power', and 'a despotic ruler would have liked to make his subjects familiar and impressed with the "true appearance" of their "lawful" monarch'.[5] But had this been the reason behind the appearance of realistic portrait of king on the coins in Asia, the native rulers of these regions would have initiated the practice of displaying their realistic portrait on their coins,

1 P K Agrawala, The Shaḍaṅga Canons of Painting, *Prāgdhārā* 1, (1990-1991), pp. 109-114.

2 N R Ray, *An Approach to Indian Art*, (Chandigarh, 1974), p. 143.

3 A K Narain, *The Indo-Greeks*, (Oxford, 1957), pl. III.

4 E J Rapson, The Successors of Alexander the Great, Chapter XXII, in R J Rapson (ed), *The Cambridge History of India* 1, (reprint, Delhi, 1987), p. 487-507, on p. 499.

5 B N Mukherjee, A Plea for the Study of Art in Coinage, *Journal of the Numismatic Society of India* 43(1), (1981), pp. 1ff, on p. 4.

even before the practice was introduced by the Hellenistic rulers. Greek art is realistic, and it was, perhaps, due to this that the portrait of the king on Hellenistic coins in Asia, too, is realistic.

The absence of the realistic portrait of kings on early Indian indigenous coins may be explained in the words of Stella Kramrisch, though written in a somewhat different context : "Portraiture belongs to civilizations that fear death : Individual likeness is not wanted when it suffices for the type to continue.'[1] And the ancient Asiatics, in general, and the Indians, in particular, do not seem to have ever entertained the fear of death.

Besides, as pointed out by Heinrich Robert Zimmer, according to ancient Indian works on poetics, a human being—a man or a woman, was never to be treated as an 'individual'. A human being was expected always to act typically, according to his or her caste, profession, sex, and age, that is the human being was 'to be a type', each class trained, and expected, to react in the same way to a particular situation.[2] This principle is reflected in Indian art as well. It appears more likely that the Asiatic rulers of Greek origin, like the Seleukids, and the Graeco-Bactrians and the Indo-Greeks, were driven by a 'craving for realism (in modeling, in movement, in expression and in the scope of the subjects

---

1 Stella Kramrisch, *Indian Sculpture*, (Calcutta, 1933), p. 134.

2 Heinrich Robert Zimmer, *The Art of Indian Asia, its Mythology and Transformations*, (completed and edited by Joseph Campbell), (New York, 1955), pp. 324-325. See also Heinrich Robert Zimmer, *Philosophies of India*, (New York and London, 1951), pp. 155ff.

treated)' to begin the tradition of realistic portraiture of the king on their coins.[1]

When the early Indian die-cutter worked under the influence of the numismatic traditions of Indo-Greeks, the Kārddamaka Kshatrapas, or the Romans, he carved realistic portrait of the king on coins.[2] But usually, the depiction of kings on early Indian indigenous coins is idealized. Anatomical and physiognomical details are often blunt or missing.[3] This was not due to ignorance of human anatomy or physiognomy on the part of the ancient Indians. Suśruta, as early as the seventh-sixth centuries BC, has given full anatomical details of the human body.[4] The feature might have crept in due to defective technique of minting, or lack of skill on the part of the die-cutter, or a 'deliberate taste for the unfinished', the last especially when it is noticed that the figures depicted show boldness in handling of form, and rapidity of execution.[5]

Although the artist of ancient India had to pay attention to *sādṛiśyaṁ*, exact physical likeness was not expected of him : his main aim was to bring out the inner spirit of the personality being depicted by him.[6] Instead of adhering

---

1 B N Mukherjee, A Plea for the Study of Art in Coinage, *Journal of the Numismatic Society of India* 43(1), (1981), pp. 1ff, on p. 4.

2 *Cf* S N Dasgupta, *Fundamentals of Indian Art*, (Bombay, 1954), p. 32.

3 See, for example, B Ch Chhabra, *Catalogue of the Gupta Gold Coins of the Bayana Hoard, in the National Museum, New Delhi*, (New Delhi, 1986), pl. I. 13—reverse.

4 S N Dasgupta, *Fundamentals of Indian Art*, (Bombay, 1954), p. 24.

5 B N Mukherjee, A Plea for the Study of Art in Coinage, *Journal of the Numismatic Society of India* 43(1), (1981), pp. 1ff, on p. 12.

6 S N Dasgupta, *Fundamentals of Indian Art*, (Bombay, 1954), p. 24.

faithfully to the anatomical or physiognomical details, the artist-die-cutter tried his best to impart to the king a royal majesty through his bearing and stance. The king on Imperial Gupta gold coins is broad-chested, and has a muscular frame : he lacks the robust and earthy figure of the king on Kushāṇa coins. But still, the majesty, vigour, energy, and prowess of the Imperial Gupta emperor on coins cannot be mistaken. This is best evident in the obverse composition of the Battle-axe type of Samudragupta,[1] where the king, as A S Altekar suggests, is shown as if surveying the battle field from some vintage point. Although such a depiction cannot be said to be realistic in the ordinary sense, it is, in a way, more real than the ordinarily realistic representations, in that 'here the attention of the artist is concentrated on the abiding inner personality which forms the basis of the varying passing emotions'.[2]

In the delineation of the deities, too, the Greek and Hellenistic artist-die-cutter adhered faithfully to the human form. The Greeks gods and goddesses 'represented in themselves the ideal perfection of human beauty'; the figure of a Greek deity almost never transgressed human form (generally speaking). Actually, human beings often served as models for divine figures. There is a suggestion that Agathokleia, believed to be the wife of the Indo-Greek ruler,

1 A S Altekar, *The Coinage of the Gupta Empire*, (Corpus of Indian Coins 4), (Varanasi, 1957), pl. II. 15-17.

2 *Cf* S N Dasgupta, *Fundamentals of Indian Art*, (Bombay, 1954), p. 55.

Menander, might have served as the model for the head of Athena on a coin of her husband.[1]

On the contrary, Indian deities, though represented often in human form, were generally 'not conceived on the pattern or types of human beauty'. As a result, they might be shown with a multiplicity of heads, arms, eyes, and even legs. Śiva and Kārttikeya, on the coins of the Yaudheya tribe, are polycephalous.[2] There are images of three-legged Sadāśiva from Khajuraho,[3] and the representation of four-legged Pharro on a gold coin of Kanishka I.[4]

It is felt that this difference in the delineation of the divine form, not only on coins, but also in sculpture and painting, was due to the difference in the objective of the Indian artist: 'the plastic artist of India, in representing gods, was not to imitate the excellence or beauty of human forms, as in the case of the Greeks, but to give expression to a spiritual message

---

1 E J Rapson, The Successors of Alexander the Great, Chapter XXII, in R J Rapson (ed), *The Cambridge History of India* 1, (reprint, Delhi, 1987), p. 487-507, on p. 498.

2 Prashant Srivastava, *Aspects of Ancient Indian Numismatics*, (Delhi, 1996), pl. XI. 2 (Śiva). John Allan, *Catalogue of the Coins of Ancient India, in the British Museum, London*, (London, 1936), pl. XXXIX. 21 (Kārttikeya).

3 Ramashraya Avasthi, Unique Syncretism of the Śuddha-Śaiva and Vīra-Śaiva Sects in Khajuraho Sculptures, in S D Singh (ed), *Culture through the Ages* (Professor B N Puri Felicitation Volume), (Delhi, 1996), pp. 381-385.

4 C A Burn, A New Kushāṇa Find, *Journal of the Numismatic Society of India* 52, (1990), pp. 7-8, and figures. Also Prashant Srivastava, The Art and Iconography of a Kushāṇa Gold Coin, *Numismatic Studies* 5, (1997), pp. 43-46.

that the forms of gods were intended to impart'.[1] By showing a deity with a multiplicity of heads, eyes, arms, and legs, he imparted a supranormal, superhuman, divine character to that deity.[2] This purpose accorded him the sanction to transgress human form, and to subordinate the anatomical parts of the body in the interest of the expression of the inner life.[3] In the absence of strict adherence to anatomical details in the delineation of the human/divine form, the outline came to play a more vital rṁle : It performed an intellectual function, making knowable the object depicted.[4] When the inner character became evident from the outline itself; anatomical and physiognomical details, became, as it were, redundant. This is best illustrated by the depiction of Śiva on the *Chatreśvara* type of the Kuṇinda coins.[5] On this type, many of the anatomical details of the figure depicted may not be made out with clarity. But it is quite evident from the outline of the figure that it represents some divinity, and the identity of the deity can be established by his title *Chatreśvara* and his attributes—the *triśūla-paraśu* in his right hand, and the animal skin hanging over his left arm.

It can easily be surmised from the realistic representation of kings and queens on Seleukid, Indo-Greek and Kārddamaka Kshatrapa coins that the artist-die-

---

1 S N Dasgupta, *Fundamentals of Indian Art*, (Bombay, 1954), pp. 11, 13.

2 Heinrich Robert Zimmer, *The Art of Indian Asia, its Mythology and Transformations*, (completed and edited by Joseph Campbell), (New York, 1955), p. 28.

3 S N Dasgupta, *Fundamentals of Indian Art*, (Bombay, 1954), p. 24.

4 Stella Kramrisch, *Indian Sculpture*, (Calcutta, 1933), p. 130.

5 John Allan, *Catalogue of the Coins of Ancient India, in the British Museum, London*, (London, 1936), pl. XXIII. 12.

cutter worked in the presence of the original. References in Sanskrit literature indicate that the Indian artist often painted portraits that resembled the original very faithfully, but the portrait was seldom drawn in the presence of its original. The artist made use of the mental picture of the original he had formed in his mind.[1] A K Coomaraswamy says that 'we find it clearly recognized that the formal element in art represents a purely mental activity', *chitta-saññā*.[2] In the *Atthasālinī*, Buddhaghosha comments : 'A mental concept (*chitta-saññā*) arises in the mind of the painter, that such and such a shape (*rūpa*) must be made in such and such a way….All the various arts (*sippa*) in the world are produced in the mind'.[3] The Indian artist first visualized the form of the subject he had chosen, his mind drawing the form to itself from the *antarhṛidaya-ākāśa*, 'the immanent space in the heart'.[4] This form revealed itself to him as a

---

1 S N Dasgupta, *Fundamentals of Indian Art*, (Bombay, 1954), pp. 43, 46. *Cf* Heinrich Robert Zimmer, *The Art of Indian Asia, its Mythology and Transformations*, (completed and edited by Joseph Campbell), (New York, 1955), p. 384.

2 Ananda K Coomaraswamy, *The Transformation of Nature in Art*, (reprint, New Delhi, 2004), p. 5.

3 *Atthasālinī* of Buddhaghosha, edited by E Müller, (Pāli Text Society, London, 1897), p. 64. See Ananda K Coomaraswamy, An Early Passage on Indian Painting, *Eastern Art* 3, (1931).

4 The *Bṛihadāraṇyakopanishad* VIII. 14, refers to *ākāśa* as 'the revealer of name and aspect'. Ananda K Coomaraswamy (*The Transformation of Nature in Art*, (reprint, New Delhi, 2004), p. 174, n. 3) observes that *antar-hṛidaya-ākāśa*, 'space in the heart', 'is the totality of this ideal space at the innermost core of our being, where only the full content of life can be experienced in the immediately experienced'.

reflection (*pratibimbavat*), or a dream (*svapnavat*).[1] The artist then realized a complete self-identification with this visualized form, and the seer and the seen attained a state transcending distinction (*anayor advaita*). Such a form 'thus known in an act of non-differentiation, being held in view as long as may be necessary (*evaṁ rūpaṁ yāvad ichchhati tāvad vibhāvayet*), is the model from which he proceeds to execution in stone, pigment, or other material'.[2] That is why, in this context, *samādhi*, 'concentration', was regarded as of greater importance than *pratyaksha*, 'empirical observation or reflex registration'. When, in the *Mālavikāgnimitram* of Kālidāsa, the artist could not capture the true beauty of the original, he attributed it to *śithila samādhi*, 'a relaxation of concentration', and not to 'want of observation'.[3] The *Śukranītisāra* also prescribes that the artist should first concentrate on the form of the subject, and then execute the work of art—*dhyātvā kuryāt*,[4] 'having concentrated, he should set to work'.[5]

The use of such a mental picture, to execute the royal figure on the coin die, by the artist-die-cutter, a picture with which the artist-die-cutter had come to realize a complete

1 Ananda K Coomaraswamy, *The Transformation of Nature in Art*, (reprint, New Delhi, 2004), p. 6.

2 Ananda K Coomaraswamy, *The Transformation of Nature in Art*, (reprint, New Delhi, 2004), p. 6.

3 *Mālavikāgnimitram* II. 2.

4 *Śukranītisāra* IV. 7. 73.

5 Ananda K Coomaraswamy, *The Transformation of Nature in Art*, (reprint, New Delhi, 2004), pp. 6-7. Ananda K Commaraswamy (*ibid.*, p. 175, n. 6) says that this is applicable, not only to visual art, but also equally to literature. He cites the example of the *Rāmāyaṇa*, which was first visualized, in its entirety, by Vālmīki, and then dictated to Gaṇeśa.

self-identification, and not the actual observation of the original subject, might be one of the reasons for the rarity of realistic portraiture on early Indian indigenous coins.[1]

1 Prashant Srivastava, On the Rarity of Busts and of Realistic Portraiture on Indigenous Indian Coins, *Pañchāla* (Journal of the Pañchāla Research Institute) 10, (1998), pp. 131-134; Prashant Srivastava, Further Observations on the Rarity of Busts and of Realistic Portraiture on Early Indian Indigenous Coins, in S Z H Jafri and N R Farooqi (ed), *Pluralities of Past—Upper Gangetic Valley through the Millennium*, (New Delhi, 2012), pp. 144-151.

7

Some problems of identification of deities on coins

The reverse of coins, and, sometimes, also the obverse, is occupied by the representation of some deity. In certain cases, the iconographical features of the deity depicted are quite clear, and there is not much difficulty in identification. Problems arise when the iconographical features are not so well-defined, or the issuer allotted some obscure deity, a place on his coins.

Amphitrite. On the reverse of the coins of the Śaka-Pahlava rulers, Maues and Azes, showing Poseidon on the obverse, is found a female figure, standing facing between two vines, which she grasps with her hands. She is dressed in *chiton* and *himation.*[1] On one type of Maues,[2] she holds the vine

1 Alexander Cunningham, Coins of the Sakas, Pt 2, (reprinted from *Numismatic Chronicle* 10, 3rd series, 1890, pp. 103-172), in Alexander Cunningham, *Coins of the Indo-Scythians, Sakas, and Kushans*, (Varanasi, 1971), pl. III. 22 (Maues); *ibid.*, pl VI. 1 (Azes).

2 Alexander Cunningham, Coins of the Sakas, Pt 2, (reprinted from *Numismatic Chronicle* 10, 3rd series, 1890, pp. 103-172), in Alexander

with her left hand, while her right hand is extended towards 'a small figure advancing with outstretched arms on left'. This female has been identified, variously, as Maenad,[1] Bacchante,[2] India,[3] and yakshī.[4] However, I feel that this female figure should be identified with Amphitrite, the wife of Poseidon, in the light of the fact, that she is represented on coin only in association with Poseidon, and never alone.

Amphitrite, according to Hesiod, was one of the 50 Nereides or daughters of Neraios,[5] although she could also have been a daughter of the Okeanine, Tethys.[6] Homer expressly refers to her as '*the* mistress and proprietress of the sea, to whom belonged all foaming waves and sea-monsters'.[7] Poseidon, the son of Rhea and Kronos, saw her on the island of Naxos, while she was dancing with the other Nereides, and ravished her.[8] Amphitrite fled to the western extremity of the sea, but this was revealed to Poseidon by the

---

Cunningham, *Coins of the Indo-Scythians, Sakas, and Kushans*, (Varanasi, 1971), pl. III. 24.

1 Percy Gardner, *Catalogue of the Coins of the Greek and Scythic Kings of Bactria and India, in the British Museum, London*, (Indian reprint, New Delhi, 1971), pp. 70-71.

2 R B Whitehead, *Catalogue of the Coins in the Punjab Museum, Lahore* 1, The Indo-Greek Coins 1, (Oxford, 1914), pp. 100, 101.

3 Alexander Cunningham, Coins of the Sakas, Pt 2, (reprinted from *Numismatic Chronicle* 10, 3rd series, 1890, pp. 103-172), in Alexander Cunningham, *Coins of the Indo-Scythians, Sakas, and Kushans*, (Varanasi, 1971), p. 4.

4 John H Marshall, *Taxila* 2, (reprint, Delhi, 1975), p. 805.

5 *Hesiodi Theogonia*, 243, 254.

6 *Apollodoros Mythographus*, 1. 2. 2.

7 *Homeri Odyssea*, 3. 91; 5. 422.

8 *Homeri Odyssea*, 3. 91.

dolphins, who also persuaded the Nereid to marry Poseidon.[1] It was this marriage that established Poseidon as the ruler of the sea, and he is often referred to as 'Husband of Amphitrite of the golden spindle'.[2] Amphitrite bore to Poseidon a son, Triton,[3] and a daughter, Rhodos.

It is interesting to note that Triton, the son of Poseidon and Amphitrite, is represented on his coin type by Hippostratos,[4] the son of the Indo-Greek ruler, Nikias, who depicted Poseidon on his coin type.[5]

It might be argued as to why a sea nymph, Amphitrite, is shown on the Śaka-Pahlava coins as holding vines. But I would like to point out that, in the scene showing the courtship if Peleus and Thetis, the parents of Achilles, depicted on the 'Portland Vase', datable to the first century BC or first century AD, and presently housed in the British Museum, London, a tree with leafy boughs is shown behind Thetis,[6] who, like Amphtrite, is a Nereid and sister of the sea nymphs.[7]

It is also worthy of note, that the lower portion of the body of the small figure, shown with Amphitrite on the coin

1 Eratosthenes, *Catasterismoi*, 31.

2 Pindarus, *Olympia*, 104.

3 *Hesiodi Theogonia*, 931.

4 A N Lahiri, *Corpus of Indo-Greek Coins*, (Calcutta, 1965), pl. XXII. 7.

5 A N Lahiri, *Corpus of Indo-Greek Coins*, (Calcutta, 1965), pl.XXVII. 6.

6 Raymond V Shoder, *Masterpieces of Greek Art*, (London, *no date*), No. 83.

7 C Kerényi, *The Gods of the Greeks*, (translation from the German text by Norman Cameron, London, New York, 1951), pp. 63-65.

type of Maues mentioned above,[1] seems to resemble a fish's posterior half, and might be identified as Triton, the son of Amphitrite and Poseidon, the lower part of whose body is described as ending in a fish's tail.[2]

Maitreya Buddha. According to the Buddhist belief, when the Śākyamuni Buddha, then a *bodhisattva*, was leaving the Tuśita heaven for the Sahā world, he removed his crown, and, placing it on the head of Maitreya, prophesied that he shall be the next 'to obtain supreme and perfect Enlightenment'.[3] On the reverse of two copper coins of the Kushāṇa ruler, Kanishka I, occurs a seated figure, with the left hand in lap, and the right hand raised up in the *varadamudrā* on one coin,[4] and with both hands raised in front of breast on the other coin.[5] Part of the reverse legend has been read as *Boudo* by Alexander Cunningham,

---

1 Alexander Cunningham, Coins of the Sakas, Pt 2, (reprinted from *Numismatic Chronicle* 10, 3rd series, 1890, pp. 103-172), in Alexander Cunningham, *Coins of the Indo-Scythians, Sakas, and Kushans*, (Varanasi, 1971), pl. III. 24.

2 C Kerényi, *The Gods of the Greeks*, (translation from the German text by Norman Cameron, London, New York, 1951), p. 188, for 'half fish, half human shape' of Triton; also *ibid.*, p. 189, for such a figure of Triton. See Prashant Srivastava, On the Identification of the "Female Between Vines" on the Poseidon Type of Coins, *Journal of the Numismatic Society of India* 55, (1993), pp. 112-113.

3 Alfred Foucher, *The Life of the Buddha, according to the Ancient Texts and Monuments of India*, (reprint, New Delhi, 2003), p. 23.

4 Alexander Cunningham, Coins of the Kushans, or Great Yue-ti, Pt 3, (reprinted from *Numismatic Chronicle* 12, 3rd series, 1892, pp. 40-82), in Alexander Cunningham, *Coins of the Indo-Scythians, Sakas, and Kushans*, (Varanasi, 1971), pl. XVIII. 12.

5 Alexander Cunningham, Coins of the Kushans, or Great Yue-ti, Pt 3, (reprinted from *Numismatic Chronicle* 12, 3rd series, 1892, pp. 40-82),

on which basis, he identified the figure as that of the Śākyamuni Buddha.[1] Since then, a number of such copper coins of Kanishka have come to light.[2] B N Mukherjee read the legend as *Ametobou*, and identified the figure as that of the *dhyānī* Buddha, Amitābha.[3] But Joe Cribb read the legend on these coins as *Metrauo Boudo*,[4] which he later modified to *Metrago Boudo*, and suggested that these two coins of Kanishka I bear the figure of Maitreya Buddha.[5]

---

in Alexander Cunningham, *Coins of the Indo-Scythians, Sakas, and Kushans*, (Varanasi, 1971), pl. XVIII. 14.

1 Alexander Cunningham, Coins of the Kushans, or Great Yue-ti, Pt 3, (reprinted from *Numismatic Chronicle* 12, 3rd series, 1892, pp. 40-82), in Alexander Cunningham, *Coins of the Indo-Scythians, Sakas, and Kushans*, (Varanasi, 1971), pp. 43-44.

2 Joe Cribb, Kanishka's Buddha Image Coins Revisited, *Silk Road Art and Archaeology* 6, (1999-2000), pp. 151-189, on pp. 177ff.

3 B N Mukherjee, Amitābha on Kushāṇa Coins, *Journal of the Numismatic Society of India* 49, (1987), pp. 44-45, and plate.

4 Joe Cribb, Kanishka's Buddha Coins—The Official Iconography of Śākyamuni and Maitreya, *Journal of the International Association of Buddhist Studies* 3(2), (1980), pp. 79-88, and plates.

5 Joe Cribb, The Origin of the Buddha Image : The Numismatic Evidence, *South Asian Archaeology*, 1984, pp. 233-244; Joe Cribb, Kanishka's Buddha Image Coins Revisited, *Silk Road Art and Archaeology* 6, (1999-2000), pp. 151-189, on p. 153.

This suggestion of Cribb has the support of scholars, like J C Huntington,[1] Martha L Carter,[2] and K D Bajpai.[3]

Zero. On the reverse of the unique gold coin of the Kushāṇa king, Huvishka, is depicted the figure of a female divinity, standing to right, and wearing *chiton* and *himation*. She holds a bow in her left hand, while with her right hand she draws an arrow from a quiver at her back.[4] The legend engraved in the left field of this coin, now in the British Museum collection, is not clear, and has been read differently by various scholars, and the identification of this deity is uncertain.

---

1 J C Huntington, A Re-examination of a Kanishka Period Tetradrachm Coin Type with an Image of Metrago/Maitreya on the Reverse (Göbl 793. 1) and a Brief Notice on the Importance of the Inscription Relative to Bactro-Gandhāran Buddhist Iconography of the Period, *Journal of the International Association of Buddhist Studies* 16(2), pp. 355-374.

2 Martha L Carter, A Consideration of Some Iconographic Details of Buddha Images on Kushāṇa Coins, in Amal Kumar Jha and Sanjay Garg (ed), *Ex Moneta—Essays on Numismatics in Honour of Dr David W MacDowall* 1, (New Delhi, 1998), pp. 215-236, on pp. 215-216.

3 K D Bajpai, Bodhisattva and Buddha : The Early Iconic Forms, *Buddhist Iconography*, (Sambhota Series 2, Tibet House, New Delhi, 1989), pp. 60-68, on pp. 63-64.

4 Percy Gardner, *Catalogue of the Coins of the Greek and Scythic Kings of Bactria and India, in the British Museum, London*, (reprint, New Delhi, 1971), p. 144, pl. XXVIII. 7; Alexander Cunningham, Coins of the Kushans or Great Yue-ti, (reprinted from *Numismatic Chronicle* 12, 3rd series, 1892, pp. 98-159), in Alexander Cunningham, *Coins of the Indo-Scythians, Sakas, and Kushans*, (Varanasi, 1971), p. 63, pl. XXII. 17.

Franz Cumont is of the opinion that the legend should be read as *Meiro*, and suggests that this legend was placed by mistake 'with the type which closely resembles Nana as huntress'.[1] J M Rosenfeld, too, seems to be of the same view, when he says that the deity whom the legend accompanies is 'another version of Nana'.[2]

F W Thomas[3] and Alexander Cunningham[4] read this legend as *Zero*. Cunningham regards it as the rendering of Zahr, which was the Persian name for Artemis/Venus,[5] on the authority of Hesychios, who says that Zaretis is the Persian Artemis.[6] Gardner also describes the deity depicted on this

---

1 Franz Cumont, *Textes et Monuments Figurés Relatifs uax Mystères de Mithra*, (Bruxelles, 1894-99), II, p. 187, *vide* J M Rosenfeld, *The Dynastic Arts of the Kushans*, (Indian edition, New Delhi, 1993), p. 101, and p. 294, n. 119.

2 J M Rosenfeld, *The Dynastic Arts of the Kushans*, (Indian edition, New Delhi, 1993), p. 101.

3 *vide* Percy Gardner, *Catalogue of the Coins of the Greek and Scythic Kings of Bactria and India, in the British Museum, London*, (reprint, New Delhi, 1971), p. lxi. Thomas regards it as the rendering of Ceres (?).

4 Alexander Cunningham, Coins of the Kushans or Great Yue-ti, (reprinted from *Numismatic Chronicle* 12, 3rd series, 1892, pp. 98-159), in Alexander Cunningham, *Coins of the Indo-Scythians, Sakas, and Kushans*, (Varanasi, 1971), pp. 63, 97, 100.

5 Alexander Cunningham, Coins of the Kushans or Great Yue-ti, (reprinted from *Numismatic Chronicle* 12, 3rd series, 1892, pp. 98-159), in Alexander Cunningham, *Coins of the Indo-Scythians, Sakas, and Kushans*, (Varanasi, 1971), pp. 63, 97, 100.

6 *Vide* Alexander Cunningham, Coins of the Kushans or Great Yue-ti, (reprinted from *Numismatic Chronicle* 12, 3rd series, 1892, pp. 98-159), in Alexander Cunningham, *Coins of the Indo-Scythians, Sakas, and Kushans*, (Varanasi, 1971), p. 63.

coin as 'Artemis',[1] but suggests that the legend is intended for *Meiro*.[2]

But Marc Aurel Stein felt that a more appropriate reading of the legend engraved on this coin would be *Teiro*, and on the basis of this legend, he proposed to identify the deity with the Zoroastrian divinity, Tishtrya, to whom is dedicated the Tir Yasht in the *Avesta*.[3] In that yasht, Tishtrya, the star Sirius, is the leader of the stars, established 'as a lord and overseer above all stars' by Ahuramazda himself.[4] Rain is regarded as a gift of Tishtrya to man.[5] The deity flies towards Vourukasha, 'the earth-surrounding Ocean',[6] as swiftly as the arrow shot by Erekhsha from Mount Khshaotha to fix the boundary between Iran and Turan,[7] and brings rain to the

1 Percy Gardner, *Catalogue of the Coins of the Greek and Scythic Kings of Bactria and India, in the British Museum, London*, (reprint, New Delhi, 1971), p. 144.

2 Percy Gardner, *Catalogue of the Coins of the Greek and Scythic Kings of Bactria and India, in the British Museum, London*, (reprint, New Delhi, 1971), p. lxi.

3 Marc Aurel Stein, Zoroastrian Deities on Indo-Scythian Coins, *Indian Antiquary* 17, (1888), p. 93.

4 Yasht VIII. 44; James Darmesteter, *The Zend Avesta* 2, *Sacred Books of the East* 23, (reprint, Delhi, 2000), p. 105.

5 Yasht VIII. 1; Darmesteter, *The Zend Avesta* 2, *Sacred Books of the East* 23, (reprint, Delhi, 2000), p. 93.

6 This ocean is sometimes regarded as the celestial ocean, but sometimes identified with the Arabian Sea. See Darmesteter, *The Zend Avesta* 2, *Sacred Books of the East* 23, (reprint, Delhi, 2000), p. 96, n. 3.

7 Yasht VIII. 6, 37; Darmesteter, *The Zend Avesta* 2, *Sacred Books of the East* 23, (reprint, Delhi, 2000), pp. 94-95, 103.

earth to fertilize the soil.[1] The yasht dedicated to Tishtrya is called Tir Yasht, and *tir* in Pahlavi and Persian means an 'arrow'. Stein feels that the Kushāṇa die-cutter modelled Tishtrya after the Greek type of Artemis, who holds the bow and arrow,[2] that is Tishtrya on this coin of Huvishka is shown in the guise of Artemis.[3] This view of Stein has been supported by André Maricq.[4]

Some scholars, however, do not agree with the view of Stein on the grounds that he 'has stretched the argument too far'.[5] They feel that as the deity is labelled as *Zero*, which seems to correspond to Zahr the Persian name for Artemis/Venus, and as the representation of the deity on the coin is modelled after the figure of Artemis on Indo-Greek coins, she should be identified as the Zoroastrian Zahr.[6]

I would like to put forth some more reasons, which render the view identifying the deity depicted on this coin with Tishtrya, difficult to accept. First, Tishtrya in the *Avesta*

---

1 Yasht VIII. 1; Darmesteter, *The Zend Avesta* 2, *Sacred Books of the East* 23, (reprint, Delhi, 2000), p. 93. *Cf Bundahishn*, VII. 2ff; E W West, *Pahlavi Texts* 1, *Sacred Books of the East* 5, (reprint, Delhi, 1993), pp. 26ff.

2 A N Lahiri, *Corpus of Indo-Greek Coins*, (Calcutta, 1965), pl. XII. 8 (coin of Demetrios).

3 Marc Aurel Stein, Zoroastrian Deities on Indo-Scythian Coins, *Indian Antiquary* 17, (1888), p. 93.

4 André Maricq, *La Grande Inscription de Kaniska, Journal Asiatic*, 1958, p. 427, *vide* J M Rosenfeld, *The Dynastic Arts of the Kushans*, (Indian edition, New Delhi, 1993), p. 294, n. 118.

5 Bhaskar Chattopadhyay, *Coins and Icons : A Study of Myths and Symbols in Indian Numismatic Art,* (Calcutta, 1972), p. 171.

6 Bhaskar Chattopadhyay, *Coins and Icons : A Study of Myths and Symbols in Indian Numismatic Art,* (Calcutta, 1972), p. 171.

is a male deity,[1] while the deity represented on the coin of Huvishka is female. But this does not present an insuperable obstacle in identifying this deity with Tishtrya, for, the Kushāṇa die-cutter, while depicting deities on the reverse of the coins, has sometimes not been very careful as regards their sex and/or iconographical features. A case in point is the representation of Selene on Kushāṇa coins. In Greek mythology, Selene is a female deity, the daughter of the Titan Hyperion and the Titaness Theia, and the sister of the sun god Helios.[2] But on Kushāṇa coins, the deity labelled as *Selene* is male,[3] and seems to be modelled after the Zoroastrian male moon god, Mao.[4]

Secondly, much has been made of the arrow shown in the hand of the deity on the coin of Huvishka, and the fact that the yasht dedicated to Tishtrya is named the Tir Yasht in which the deity is associated with an arrow (*tir* in Pahlavi and Persian).[5] But it must be noted that it is not the god himself who is likened to an arrow in the yasht, but his swiftness with which he moves towards Vourukasha.[6] The yasht very

---

1 Yasht VIII, Darmesteter, *The Zend Avesta* 2, *Sacred Books of the East* 23, (reprint, Delhi, 2000), pp. 92ff.

2 C Kerényi, *The Gods of the Greeks*, (London, 1951), pp. 190ff.

3 Percy Gardner, *Catalogue of the Coins of the Greek and Scythic Kings of Bactria and India, in the British Museum, London*, (reprint, New Delhi, 1971), pl. XXVI. 1.

4 Percy Gardner, *Catalogue of the Coins of the Greek and Scythic Kings of Bactria and India, in the British Museum, London*, (reprint, New Delhi, 1971), pl. XXVI. 9; pl. XXVII. 18; etc.

5 See above. The imagery of the arrow may also be hinted at in the statement of the Tir Yasht (Yasht VIII. 2) that the 'shining, undefiled rays' of [the star] Tishtrya pierce 'from afar'.

6 Yasht VIII. 6, 37; Darmesteter, *The Zend Avesta* 2, *Sacred Books of the East* 23, (reprint, Delhi, 2000), pp. 94-95, 103.

clearly states that Tishtrya flew towards Vourukasha, '*as swiftly as* the arrow...which Erekhsha...shot from Mount Khshaotha to Mount Hvanvant'.[1] Thus, Tishtrya did not fly towards Vourukasha in the *form* of an arrow. In fact, the yasht explicitly states that when he flew towards that ocean, he took the shape of 'a white, beautiful horse, with golden ears and golden caparison'.[2]

Further, on the coin, the deity is shown in the posture of attack, with a bow held in her left hand, while with her right hand she draws an arrow from the quiver at her back. But nowhere in the Tir Yasht is Tishtrya described as using bow and arrow to worst his enemy or enemies. In fact, when his struggle with Apaosha, the daëva of drought, is described in the yasht, the deity takes the form of a white horse, while his rival, that of a dark horse,[3] and when they meet in combat, they fight 'hoof against hoof'.[4] In the yasht, Tishtrya is described as assuming various shapes, like that of a man

---

1 Yasht VIII. 6; Darmesteter, *The Zend Avesta* 2, *Sacred Books of the East* 23, (reprint, Delhi, 2000), pp. 94-95 (italics mine).

2 Yasht VIII. 20, 26, 30, 46; Darmesteter, *The Zend Avesta* 2, *Sacred Books of the East* 23, (reprint, Delhi, 2000), pp. 99, 100ff, 106.

3 Yasht VIII. 20-22, 26-28; Darmesteter, *The Zend Avesta* 2, *Sacred Books of the East* 23, (reprint, Delhi, 2000), pp. 99, 100ff. *Cf Bundahishn*, VII. 7-8; E W West, *Pahlavi Texts* 1, *Sacred Books of the East* 5, (reprint, Delhi, 1993), p. 27.

4 Yasht VIII. 22, 28; Darmesteter, *The Zend Avesta* 2, *Sacred Books of the East* 23, (reprint, Delhi, 2000), pp. 99, 100.

fifteen years of age,[1] a golden-horned bull,[2] or a horse,[3] but never that of an arrow.

From the above, it would appear that in the present state of our knowledge, it is not appropriate to accept the view that the deity represented on the coin of Huvishka under discussion here should be identified with the Zoroastrian divinity, Tishtrya. It seems more likely that the Kushāṇa die-cutter has here depicted the Iranian deity Zahr, modelling her after her Greek counterpart, Artemis.[4]

---

1 Yasht VIII. 13-14; Darmesteter, *The Zend Avesta* 2, *Sacred Books of the East* 23, (reprint, Delhi, 2000), pp. 97-98. See *Bundahishn*, VII. 4; E W West, *Pahlavi Texts* 1, *Sacred Books of the East* 5, (reprint, Delhi, 1993), p. 26.

2 Yasht VIII. 16; Darmesteter, *The Zend Avesta* 2, *Sacred Books of the East* 23, (reprint, Delhi, 2000), p. 98.

3 Yasht VIII. 18; Darmesteter, *The Zend Avesta* 2, *Sacred Books of the East* 23, (reprint, Delhi, 2000), p. 98. Also, see above, for Tishtrya assuming the shape of a white horse when he flew towards Vourukasha to give combat to Apaosha.

4 Prashant Srivastava, Zero (?) on the Gold Coin of Huvishka : Some Observations, in *Bulletin of Museums and Archaeology in UP*, (forthcoming).

8

Some enigmatic types

There are certain coin-types, the interpretation of which has baffled numismatists and historians alike. Quite often, it is felt that correct interpretation of these coin-types might have an important bearing on the reconstruction of the history of a dynasty, region, or period.

Hermaios-Kalliope type. The fact, that nearly three dozen Indo-Greek rulers, known mainly from numismatic sources, have to be placed within a period of merely two centuries, and that, too, mainly in northwestern India, seems to indicate that the region under the Indo-Greeks was divided into several principalities, with several princes, belonging to different families, ruling simultaneously over the various principalities. There is evidence, both literary[1] and numismatic, of internecine warfare between these rival Indo-Greek families. R B Whitehead observes in this connection :

1 Eg, Justin writes about the struggle between Eukratides and the Euthydemids; also the evidence of the Yugapurāṇa section of the *Gārgīsaṁhitā*, *vide* H C Raychaudhuri, *Political History of Ancient India*, (7th ed, Calcutta, 1972), p. 343, n. 3.

'We get an impression of the simultaneous rule of more than one king, of mutual antagonism, confusion, and civil war. The Yavanas seem to have been their own worst enemies.'[1] This civil war must have told heavily upon the power of the Indo-Greek princes. It was only when the nomadic tribes—the Śaka-Pahlavas, started overthrowing them in different regions, by taking advantage of their weakness, arising out of internecine warfare, that the rival Indo-Greek families appear to have made a bid for alliance against the Śaka-Pahlava menace.

There is a type of double-*decadrachms*, struck by Amyntas, bearing, on the obverse, the bust of the king in smooth helmet, to the right, and, on the reverse, enthroned Zeus, holding out Athena on his outstretched right hand, with the Greek legend, *Basileos nikatoros Amyntou*.[2] The device of 'enthroned Zeus' on the reverse of this type has associations with the Eukratids,[3] while the device of Athena, shown on the outstretched right hand of Zeus on the reverse of this type, has associations with Menander and his successors.[4] This has led A K Narain to suggest that Amyntas had formed some sort of an alliance with some successor of Apollodotos, against the common danger of the nomadic invaders.[5] This successor of Apollodotos, who entered into an alliance with Amyntas, would have been Zoilos II or Apollophanes, for the reverse

1 R B Whitehead, Notes on Indo-Greek Coins, *Numismatic Chronicle*, 1923, pp. 294ff, on p. 308.

2 A K Narain, Remarkable Discovery of Some Indo-Greek Victory Medallions, *Journal of the Numismatic Society of India* 15(2), (1953), p. 213, pl. IX. 1.

3 A K Narain, *The Indo-Greeks*, (Oxford, 1957), p. 157.

4 A K Narain, *The Indo-Greeks*, (Oxford, 1957), p. 157.

5 A K Narain, *The Indo-Greeks*, (Oxford, 1957), p. 157.

of some of their respective monetary issues depict Athena.[1] This alliance appears to be the first step towards uniting the resources of these two rival Indo-Greek factions, to combat the danger posed by the nomadic Śaka-Pahlavas.

Another step in this direction seems to be the marriage of Hermaios, believed to be the son of Amyntas,[2] with Kalliope, believed to be the daughter of Hippostratos.[3] This Hippostratos is believed to be a descendant of Antimachos I.[4] The source of our knowledge about this matrimonial alliance is a coin type, in silver, based on the Indian standard, round in shape, and bearing the conjugate busts of Hermaios and Kalliope to the right on the obverse; the reverse has the helmeted and diademed king mounted on a prancing horse to the right. The Greek legend on the obverse reads *Basaileos soteros Ermaiou kai Kalliope*, while the Kharoshṭhī legend on the reverse reads *Maharajasa tratarasa Heramayasa Kaliyapaya* (coin no. 51).[5] Thus, the Greek legend on the obverse and the Kharoshṭhī legend on the reverse, both mention the names of the king and the queen, but the titles of *basileus* and *soteros*, rendered into Prakrit as *maharaja* and

1 R B Whitehead, *Catalogue of the Coins in the Punjab Museum, Lahore* 1, The Indo-Greek Coins, (Oxford, 1914), pp. 65-67, pl. VII. 534 (Zoilos II); *ibid.*, p. 68, pl. VII. 550 (Apollophanes).

2 W W Tarn, *The Greeks in Bactria and India*, (reprint, New Delhi, 1980), p. 331; A K Narain, *The Indo-Greeks*, (Oxford, 1957), p. 181, chart.

3 W W Tarn, *The Greeks in Bactria and India*, (reprint, New Delhi, 1980), p. 337; A K Narain, *The Indo-Greeks*, (Oxford, 1957), p. 181, chart.

4 A K Narain, *The Indo-Greeks*, (Oxford, 1957), p. 181, chart.

5 Percy Gardner, *Catalogue of the Coins of the Greek and Scythic Kings of Bactria and India, in the British Museum, London*, (reprint, New Delhi, 1971), p. 66, pl. XV. 9, 10.

tratara, are used only for Hermaios. R C Senior has referred to a rare joint issue of Hermaios and Kalliope, on which the device of king mounted on a prancing horse occupies the obverse, replacing the conjugate busts of the king and the queen.[1]

The fact that the figure or emblem of some divinity, which usually occupies the reverse of the Indo-Greek coins, is here replaced by the device of 'King on prancing horse', which occurs on the reverse of some of the silver issues of rulers, like Antimachos II,[2] Philoxenos,[3] Menander II,[4] and Hippostratos,[5] of the family of Antimachos I,[6] when considered together with another fact, that on a series of the silver coins struck by Hermaios separately, the device of 'King on prancing horse' occurs on the obverse, in place of the usual royal bust,[7] reveals the significance of the Hermaios-Kalliope coin types.

On the basis of the reverse device of 'King on prancing horse', found on the Hermaios-Kalliope type, Alexander

---

1 See Prashant Srivastava, *Encyclopaedia of Indian Coins (Ancient Coins of Northern India, up to* circa *650 AD)* 1, (Delhi, 2012), p. 193.

2 A N Lahiri, *Corpus of Indo-Greek Coins*, (Calcutta, 1965), pl. VI. 10.

3 A N Lahiri, *Corpus of Indo-Greek Coins*, (Calcutta, 1965), pl. XXVII. 3.

4 A N Lahiri, *Corpus of Indo-Greek Coins*, (Calcutta, 1965), pl. XXVI. 10.

5 A N Lahiri, *Corpus of Indo-Greek Coins*, (Calcutta, 1965), pl. XXII. 8.

6 That these kings belonged to the Family of Antimachos, see A K Narain, *The Indo-Greeks*, (Oxford, 1957), p. 181, chart.

7 A N Lahiri, *Corpus of Indo-Greek Coins*, (Calcutta, 1965), pp. 140-141, pl. XXI. 9.

Cunningham had suggested that Kalliope might have been a descendant of Antimachos.[1] The fact, that she is shown wearing a diadem on these coins, is evidence enough to prove that she would have been a princess in her own right.[2] As such, Cunningham's suggestion, that the joint issues of Hermaios and Kalliope 'refer to a royal alliance' between the families of Antimachos and Eukratides, seems to be quite convincing, and has come to be accepted by a vast majority of scholars.[3]

The marriage of Hermaios with Kalliope was of great political significance. May it be suggested that, apart from cementing the alliance forged between the two Indo-Greek royal families, it might even have led to the amalgamation of the kingdom of Hermaios, and the paternal kingdom of Kalliope ? Kalliope was, perhaps, the only issue of Hippostratos.[4] She ruled over the kingdom, which she had inherited from her father, conjointly with her husband, Hermaios, who, it must be made clear, was a king in his own right. This supposition seems to explain, satisfactorily, the joint coins of Hermaios and Kalliope. Hermaios was the ruler of his own kingdom, apart from being the co-ruler of

1 Alexander Cunningham, *Coins of Alexander's Successors in the East*, (reprint, Varanasi, 1970), p. 94.

2 W W Tarn, *The Greeks in Bactria and India*, (reprint, New Delhi, 1980), p. 337.

3 E J Rapson, The Successors of Alexander the Great, Chapter XXII, in R J Rapson (ed), *The Cambridge History of India* 1, (reprint, Delhi, 1987), p. 487-507, on pp. 493, 505; W W Tarn, *The Greeks in Bactria and India*, (reprint, New Delhi, 1980), p. 337; A K Narain, *The Indo-Greeks*, (Oxford, 1957), pp. 161-162.

4 Hippostratos appears to have been the last ruler of the family of Antimachos I. See A K Narain, *The Indo-Greeks*, (Oxford, 1957), p. 181, chart.

the kingdom which Kalliope had inherited from her father, while Kalliope was the co-ruler of the latter kingdom only. Hence, the name and titles of Hermaios, before the name of Kalliope, and 'King on prancing horse', the device of the ancestors of Kalliope, occupy the reverse of these joint coins.

It might also be suggested that, after some time, when Hermaios had consolidated his position in the kingdom, which Kalliope had inherited from her father, he removed her name and bust from his monetary issues. It is also possible that she had died by that time. The first issue of Hermaios after this would appear to be the one bearing the device of 'King on prancing horse', on the obverse.[1] The issue of these coins seems to have been an attempt, on the part of Heraios, to make his rule alone acceptable to the people of the kingdom, which Kalliope had inherited from Hippostratos, and over which she had ruled as a co-ruler with Hermaios.[2]

Sātakarṇi I-Nāganikā type. A silver coin, bearing the names of Sātakarṇi I and Nāganikā, is believed to be the earliest known silver coin of the Sātavāhanas.[3] The obverse

---

1 A N Lahiri, *Corpus of Indo-Greek Coins*, (Calcutta, 1965), pp. 140-141, pl. XXI. 9. *Cf* E T Newell, *Miscellanea Numismatics—Cyrene to India*, (Numismatic Notes and Monographs of the American Numismatic Society 82, New York, 1937), p. 89, who regards this type as 'among Hermaeus' earliest issues and soon replaced by his far commoner coins adorned with the royal portrait on the obverse'.

2 Prashant Srivastava, Some Observations on the Hermaios-Kalliope Type, *Journal of the Numismatic Society of India* 52, (1990), pp. 45-47.

3 V V Mirashi, *Sātavāhanoṁ aura Paśchimī Kshatrapoṁ kā Itihāsa aura Abhilekha*, (Hindi), (Lucknow, 1982), Pt 1, p. 224.

of the coin bears the figure of a horse,[1] with the head off the flan, on the left, and a two-line Brāhmī legend, *Raṁño-siri-Sāta[ka]/Nāganikāya*. The reverse has an Ujjain symbol with a *svastika* in each orb, and a pellet between the orbs; on the left is a spear-like object.[2] As the obverse legend mentions the names of both Sātakarṇi I and Nāganikā, it has been suggested that the coin type was a joint issue of this Sātavāhana king and his queen.[3] V V Mirashi is the view that this joint issue shows that Nāganikā had great influence and power in the government of the Sātavāhana kingdom.[4]

There is, however, some controversy regarding the relationship between Sātakarṇi I and Nāganikā. The latter is usually regarded as the queen of Sātakarṇi I by most of the scholars. S L Katare, however, suggests that she was the mother of Sātakarṇi I,[5] as the figure of Nāganikā is seen before that of Sātakarṇi I at Naneghat. It has also been

---

1 Mala Dutta (*A Study of the Sātavāhana Coinage*, New Delhi, 1990, p. 269, Type XVI) writes, 'horse (or lion ?)'.

2 P J Chinmulgund, A Unique Silver Coin of Sātakarṇi and Nāganikā, *Journal of the Numismatic Society of India* 38(1), (1976), pp. 6-11, on pp. 6-7, pl. I. 3. Also V V Mirashi, *Sātavāhanoṁ aura Paśchimī Kshatrapoṁ kā Itihāsa aura Abhilekha*, (Hindi), (Lucknow, 1982), Pt 1, pp. 223-224, pl. 20. 33 (obverse only).

3 V V Mirashi, *Sātavāhanoṁ aura Paśchimī Kshatrapoṁ kā Itihāsa aura Abhilekha*, (Hindi), (Lucknow, 1982), Pt 1, pp. 13, 16, 19, 223-224; *ibid.*, p. 9.

4 V V Mirashi, *Sātavāhanoṁ aura Paśchimī Kshatrapoṁ kā Itihāsa aura Abhilekha*, (Hindi), (Lucknow, 1982), Pt 1, p. 224.

5 S L Katare, King Sātavāhana of the Coins, *Indian Historical Quarterly* 27, pp. 210-214, on p. 213; also Two Unique Coins of Sātavāhana Sātakarṇi I, *Journal of the Numismatic Society of India* 13, (1951), pp. 35-39, on pp. 35ff.

suggested that she acted as a queen-regent for her son.[1] V V Mirashi, however, rules this out. He suggests that the image of Nāganikā was sculpted, before that of the king, because of the prestige in which the queen was held.[2] He takes the discovery, from Junnar, of this coin, bearing the names of Sātakarṇi I and Nāganikā, as proof of Nāganikā's being the wife of Sātakarṇi I.[3] P J Chinmulgund, who first published this coin, also used the evidence of this coin to show that Nāganikā was the wife of Sātakarṇi I.

According to Chinmulgund[4] and Mirashi,[5] the figure of the horse, seen on the obverse of this coin, refers to the *aśvamedha*, and they suggest that this coin was issued on the occasion of the horse sacrifice performed by Sātakarṇi I. The Naneghat inscription of Nāganikā refers to the

1 S L Katare, King Sātavāhana of the Coins, *Indian Historical Quarterly* 27, pp. 210-214, on p. 213; also Two Unique Coins of Sātavāhana Sātakarṇi I, *Journal of the Numismatic Society of India* 13, (1951), pp. 35-39, on pp. 35ff.

2 V V Mirashi says that the Naneghat inscription of Nāganikā reveals her importance, and the awe in which she was held. See V V Mirashi, *Sātavāhanoṁ aura Paśchimī Kshatrapoṁ kā Itihāsa aura Abhilekha*, (Hindi), (Lucknow, 1982), Pt 1, p. 16.

3 It might be mentioned here that, if Nāganikā was the mother of Sātakarṇi I, and was acting as his regent, her name might be mentioned on the coins issued during the period of her regency, as seen in the case of some joint coins of the Indo-Greek queen regent, Agathokleia, and her son, Strato I. See Prashant Srivastava, *Aspects of Ancient Indian Numismatics*, (Delhi, 1996), pp. 1-15.

4 P J Chinmulgund, A Unique Silver Coin of Sātakarṇi and Nāganikā, *Journal of the Numismatic Society of India* 38(1), (1976), pp. 6-11, on pp. 9, 11.

5 V V Mirashi, *Sātavāhanoṁ aura Paśchimī Kshatrapoṁ kā Itihāsa aura Abhilekha*, (Hindi), (Lucknow, 1982), Pt 1, pp. 19, 224, Pt 2, p. 9.

performance of two *aśvamedha* sacrifices by Sātakarṇi I.[1] Chinmulgund says that the spear-like object on the reverse, which, according to him, represents the *sūchī* used by the queen during *aśvamedha*, also points at the performance of the horse sacrifice by the issuer of the coin. This *sūchī*, it has been remarked, is quite similar to that seen on the *Aśvamedha* type of Samudragupta.[2] But, while the *Aśvamedha* type of the Gupta ruler shows the figure of the chief queen on the reverse, without mentioning her name, the Sātakarṇi I-Nāganikā coin mentions the name of the queen, but her figure is not depicted on the coin.[3] Chinmulgund argues that only the *mahishī*, who had an important function to perform during the *aśvamedha*, would be represented on the coins issued on the occasion of a horse sacrifice. As the name of Nāganikā is mentioned on this coin, she can only be the queen of Sātakarṇi I. This argument seems to be quite logical, as well as forceful.

Chinmulgund does not regard the Sātakarṇi I-Nāganikā coin as a joint issue,[4] and is of the view that her name is mentioned on this coin, issued on the occasion of the *aśvamedha*, because of the part she had played as the *mahishī*

---

1 V V Mirashi, *Sātavāhanoṁ aura Paśchimī Kshatrapoṁ kā Itihāsa aura Abhilekha*, (Hindi), (Lucknow, 1982), Pt 1, p. 18. See text, line 11, *ibid.*, Pt 2, p. 11.

2 A S Altekar, *The Coinage of the Gupta Empire*, (Corpus of Indian Coins 4), (Varanasi, 1957), pl. III. 6-12.

3 See P J Chinmulgund, A Unique Silver Coin of Sātakarṇi and Nāganikā, *Journal of the Numismatic Society of India* 38(1), (1976), pp. 6-11, on p. 9. Chinmulgund also suggests that Samudragupta might have struck his *Aśvamedha* type of coins after seeing some specimens of the Sātakarṇi I-Nāganikā type during his *digvijaya*.

4 P J Chinmulgund, A Unique Silver Coin of Sātakarṇi and Nāganikā, *Journal of the Numismatic Society of India* 38(1), (1976), pp. 6-11, on p. 8.

during the sacrifice. If this be accepted, the coin is only a commemorative medallion, celebrating the *aśvamedha* performed by Sātakarṇi I. But it is equally possible that the Sātakarṇi I-Nāganikā coin is a joint issue, for it is well-known that Nāganikā was an influential person in the Sātavāhana administration. The coin may be a joint issue, as well as a commemorative medallion, issued to mark the performance of the *aśvamedha* by Sātakarṇi I.

***Di-Kshema[gupta]* type.** A large number of coins from Kashmir bear the legend, *Di-Kshema[gupta]*.[1] The occurrence of this legend is very interesting. Alexander Cunningham took this to be the contracted form of the name, *Diddākshema*,[2] by which King Kshemagupta of Kashmir had come to be called due to his infatuation for his queen, Diddā, as reported by Kalhaṇa.[3] But S K Maity, very pertinently, asks, '...could the prerogative to issue coins be so lightly treated as to allow a queen's name to appear simply because the king was infatuated by her beauty ?'[4]

---

1 Alexander Cunningham, *Coins of Mediaeval India*, (reprint, Delhi, 1967), p. 45, pl. IV. 11; V A Smith, *Coins of Ancient India—Catalogue of the Coins in the Indian Museum, Calcutta, including the Cabinet of the Asiatic Society of Bengal* 1, (reprint, Varanasi, 1972), p. 270, pl. XXVII. 10.

2 Alexander Cunningham, *Coins of Mediaeval India*, (reprint, Delhi, 1967), p. 45, n. 21.

3 *Rājataraṅgiṇī*, *Taraṅga* VI, verse 177, English translation by R S Pandit, p. 244 : 'As his mind became absorbed in Diddā, the daughter of the Śāhi, the king came to be known by the humiliating epithet of Diddākshema.'

4 S K Maity, *Early Indian Coins and Currency System*, (New Delhi, 1970), p. 8.

V A Smith takes these coins as the joint issues of Kshemagupta and Diddā.[1] But the appearance of the name of the queen before that of the king is difficult to explain. It would have been understandable, had Kshemagupta attained royalty because of his marriage with Diddā. But he was a king in his own right, and had inherited the kingdom from his father, Parvagupta.[2] His matrimonial alliance with the Loharas and the Śāhis, with whom Diddā was related, might have provided stability to his rule in Kashmir.[3] But that, too, cannot possibly account for the occurrence of the name of Diddā before that of the king on the coins, unless the Loharas and the Śāhis had insisted upon the joint rule of Diddā with Kshemagupta, with Diddā as the senior co-ruler.

After the death of Kshemagupta, his son, Abhimanyu, was placed on the throne, but with Diddā acting as the regent. Abhimanyu was followed on the throne by his sons, Nandigupta, Tribhuvana, and Bhānugupta, one after the other. All of them were killed by Diddā, who finally ascended the throne in 980 AD, and ruled till 1003 AD, when she died after appointing her nephew, Saṁgrāmarāja of Lohara, as her successor. During all these years, right from the beginning of her regency after the death of Kshemagupta, Diddā had to face several rebellions, which she crushed with

---

1 V A Smith, *Coins of Ancient India—Catalogue of the Coins in the Indian Museum, Calcutta, including the Cabinet of the Asiatic Society of Bengal* 1, (reprint, Varanasi, 1972), p. 270 : 'Kshemagupta *with* Queen Diddā'.

2 See D C Ganguly, Central and Western India, Chapter V, in R C Majumdar, A D Pusalker, and A K Majumdar (ed), *The Age of Imperial Kanauj*, (The History and Culture of the Indian People 4), (Bombay, 1984), pp. 83-132, on p. 120.

3 K S Saksena, *Political History of Kashmir*, pp. 142-144.

an iron hand.[1] Y B Singh suggests that *Diddākshema* of the *Rājataraṅgiṇī* does not stand for *Diddāyaḥ-Kshemagupta*, 'Kshemagupta of Diddā', as suggested by Kalhaṇa, but for *Diddā-Kshemaguptau*, 'Diddā of Kshemagupta'. He says that *Di-Kshema[gupta]* on these coins does not show the infatuation of Kshemagupta for his queen, but that by referring to herself as 'Diddā of Kshemagupta', the queen is trying 'to convince the people that she was ruling the valley by the right of her husband and not by the right of her father or maternal grandfather with whom people of the valley were annoyed'.[2] The hypothesis is quite convincing, and we have the example of the Indo-Greeks, and of the Kushāṇa ruler, Kujula Kadphises, issuing commemorative medals to appeal to the memory of earlier historical personages from whom they claimed descent, thus proclaiming their right to sovereignty. But the major problem in accepting this conjecture of Y B Singh is the worthless character of Kshemagupta. If the testimony of the *Rājataraṅgiṇī* is to be accepted, Kshemagupta was a man given to the pleasures of the senses.[3] Kalhaṇa is full of contempt for this king, and scholars regard his eight year reign as an inglorious one.[4]

1 See D C Ganguly, Central and Western India, Chapter V, in R C Majumdar, A D Pusalker, and A K Majumdar (ed), *The Age of Imperial Kanauj* (The History and Culture of the Indian People 4), (Bombay, 1984), pp. 83-132, on pp. 120-121.

2 Y B Singh, Legend Diddākshema : A Riddle Explained, *Journal of the Numismatic Society of India* 46, (1984), pp. 107-110, on p. 109.

3 See *Rājataraṅgiṇī*, *Taraṅga* VI, verses 150-183, English translation by R S Pandit, pp. 241-245.

4 See D C Ganguly, Central and Western India, Chapter V, in R C Majumdar, A D Pusalker, and A K Majumdar (ed), *The Age of Imperial Kanauj* (The History and Culture of the Indian People 4), (Bombay, 1984), pp. 83-132, on p. 120.

Would appealing to the memory of such a ruler have helped the cause of Diddā, and evoked the sympathy of the people of Kashmir ? I find is highly improbable. It is difficult to perceive the inhabitants of the valley of Kashmir supporting the cause of a cruel and unchaste dowager, because she had appealed to the memory of her husband, who himself was a man committed to the pleasures of the senses. The credit for Diddā's remaining in power for such a long period of time goes to her own tact and skill.

Could it be that, just as the Lichchhavis are believed to have insisted upon having Kumāradevī as their representative in the joint rule of Chandragupta I and Kumāradevī, the Loharas and the Śāhis also insisted upon the joint rule of Kshemagupta and Diddā in Kashmir, where they had helped stabilize the rule of Kshemagupta, but with Diddā as the senior co-ruler ? This, I think, would explain the presence of the initial of the name of Diddā occurring before the full name of Kshemagupta, on the coins. The presence of the coins, issued in the name of Diddā alone, would seem to support this contention.[1]

Yet another possibility is that Kshemagupta, being infatuated by the beauty of Diddā, rejoiced in having her name prefixed to his own name. The epithet, which Kalhaṇa, at a later date, refers to as 'humiliating', might actually have been coined by the flatterers, who are reported to have surrounded

1 Alexander Cunningham, *Coins of Mediaeval India*, (reprint, Delhi, 1967), p. 45, pl. IV. 16; V A Smith, *Coins of Ancient India—Catalogue of the Coins in the Indian Museum, Calcutta, including the Cabinet of the Asiatic Society of Bengal* 1, (reprint, Varanasi, 1972), p. 271, pl. XXVII. 13.

Kshemagupta,[1] to please him, or by the king himself, and he introduced this epithet on coins, just to proclaim his love for his queen, and not due to joint rule.[2]

Pṛithvīrāja III-Mohammad *bin* Sāmī type. A coin bearing the name of Mohammad *bin* Sāmī on one side, and that of Pṛithvīrāja III Chāhamāna on the other, was brought to light by H Nelson-Wright.[3] Nelson-Wright is of the view that the coin was issued by the Muslim conqueror, 'as a suzerain of Pṛthvīrāja of Ajmer'. He takes it as a joint issue, commenting that 'No. 36-A shows the transition stage, the obverse bearing the name of the conqueror and the reverse that of the conquered Pṛthvīrāja'.[4] D C Sircar, however, points out that, usually, a ruler is not obliged to mention on his coins, the name of his subordinate ruler. As such, it is only natural to think that this coin was issued by a subordinate ruler. But who, among the two, was a subordinate ruler ? Sircar writes: 'Unfortunately the known facts of the relations between the said two rulers do not speak of any period when one of them could have issued coins as a subordinate of the other.'[5]

---

1 See *Rājataraṅgiṇī*, *Taraṅga* VI, verse 152, English translation by R S Pandit, p. 241.

2 Prashant Srivastava, *Joint Coin-types of Ancient India*, (Numismatic Notes and Monographs of he Numismatic Society of India 22), (Varanasi, 1990), pp. 8-9.

3 H Nelson-Wright, *The Coinage and Metrology of the Sultāns of Dehlī, incorporating a Catalogue of the Coins in the Author's Cabinet now in the Dehlī Museum*, (Delhi, 1936), p. 12, no. 36-A.

4 H Nelson-Wright, *The Coinage and Metrology of the Sultāns of Dehlī, incorporating a Catalogue of the Coins in the Author's Cabinet now in the Dehlī Museum*, (Delhi, 1936), p. 12, no. 36-A.

5 D C Sircar, *Studies in Indian Coins*, (Delhi, 1968), p. 230.

Kunwar Devi Singh has suggested that this type was issued by the Muslim conqueror, as he considered it wise to retain on his coin type, the name of Pṛithvīrāja III, at least for the time being, to make his coins popular.[1]

P L Gupta has suggested that Śāhi coins, having a recumbent bull on one side and a horseman on the other, were copied by the Ghaznavids, the Chāhamānas, and the Tomaras. These rulers mention the name of the issuing monarch on the horseman side, and the legend, *Śrī-sāmantadeva*, on the recumbent bull side. On the coins of Pṛithvīrājadeva, while the bull side has the legend, *Āśāvarī-Śrī-sāmantadeva*, the issues of Mohammad *bin* Sāmī have the legend, *Śrī-Hammīra*, the Indianized form of the Sultan's title, *amir*, on the horseman side. P L Gupta is of the view that, on the coin bearing the names of Mohammad *bin* Sāmī and Pṛithvīrāja III, the name of the Chāhamāna ruler occurred owing to a mistake on the part of the mint officers. This mistake was soon detected and rectified by replacing the name of Pṛithvīrāja III with the title of Mohammad *bin* Sāmī.[2] While A S Altekar supports this view,[3] D C Sircar does not favour P L Gupta's suggestion.[4]

---

1 Kunwar Devi Singh, *Pṛithvirāja aura Mohammad Ghorī kā Saṁyukta Sikkā*, (Hindi), in *Nāgarī Prachāriṇī Patrikā* 57, pp. 59-60; P L Gupta, Summary of the article of Kunwar Devi Singh, *Journal of the Numismatic Society of India* 14, (1952), p. 147.

2 P L Gupta's comment on Kunwar Devi Singh, *Pṛithvīrāja aura Mohammad Ghorī kā Saṁyukta Sikkā*, (Hindi), in *Nāgarī Prachāriṇī Patrikā* 57, pp. 270-273.

3 A S Altekar, Editor's note on D C Sircar, A Coin of Muhammad Bin Sām and Pṛithvīrāja, *Journal of the Numismatic Society of India* 15(2), (1953), pp. 229-235, on pp. 234-235.

4 See D C Sircar, *Studies in Indian Coins*, (Delhi, 1968), pp. 233-237.

He says that this can be possible only if the type was issued by a private agency.[1]

On the basis of the evidence of the *Tāja-ul-ma'asir* of Hasan Nizāmī, Dasaratha Sharma suggests that Pṛithvīrāja III Chāhamāna, after his defeat in the battle of Tarain in 1192 AD, might have served for a short time as a vassal of Mohammad *bin* Sāmī, and the coin bearing the names of both Pṛithvīrāja and Mohammad *bin* Sāmī might have been issued during that period.[2] But D C Sircar rejects this suggestion,[3] in the light of the information supplied by the *Hammīramahākāvya* : 'When Udayarāja, a great friend and ally of Pṛthvīrāja, heard of his captivity, he sat down before Delhi and besieged it. During the siege, a courtier of the Ghūrī Sultān suggested to his master that it would be becoming on his part to release the Cauhān. Muizuddīn, it is said, was so incensed by the proposal, that he denounced the advisor as a traitor and ordered Pṛthvīrāja to be imprisoned in the citadel where, a few days afterwards, he breathed his last.'[4]

In view of the above, D C Sircar, very rightly, observes: 'We admit that the real significance of the coin under study is not very easy to explain and is likely to remain doubtful until further evidence on the point is forthcoming.'[5]

---

1 D C Sircar, *Studies in Indian Coins*, (Delhi, 1968), pp. 233-236.

2 Dasharatha Sharma, Coin of Muhammad Bin Sām and Pṛithvīrāja, *Journal of the Numismatic Society of India* 16, (1954), p. 122.

3 D C Sircar, *Studies in Indian Coins*, (Delhi, 1968), p. 237.

4 *Hammīramahākāvya* of Nayachandra Sūri, edited by N J Kirtane, (Bombay, 1879), Introduction, pp. 20-21.

5 D C Sircar, *Studies in Indian Coins*, (Delhi, 1968), p. 236. See Prashant Srivastava, *Joint Coin-types of Ancient India*, (Numismatic Notes and Monographs of the Numismatic Society of India 22), (Varanasi, 1990), pp. 9-10.

9

Monograms on coins

Certain monograms, comprising Greek, and sometimes even Kharoshṭhī, letters, occur on Indo-Greek and Śaka-Pahlava coins (for example, coin no. 52). The significance of these monograms on coins is a matter of debate among scholars. Bayer suggested that they represent dates.[1] But, as pointed out by H H Wilson, a single monogram may occur on the coins of several rulers, and, hence, cannot be treated as a date.[2] K W Dobbins' attempt, to associate the different monograms with mints and coin series,[3] has also failed to yield concrete results. Alexander Cunningham was of the

---

1 T S Bayer, *Historia Regni Graecorum Bactriani*, (St Petersbourg, 1738), *vide* A N Lahiri, *Corpus of Indo-Greek Coins*, (Calcutta, 1965), p. 53.

2 H H Wilson, *Ariana Antiqua—A Descriptive Account of the Antiquites and Coins of Afghanistan*, (reprint, Delhi, 1971), p. 238.

3 K W Dobbins, *Śaka-Pahlava Coinage*, (Memoirs of the Numismatic Society of India 5), (Varanasi, 1973), pp. 121-130; K W Dobbins, *A Schema of Indo-Baktrian Coinage*, (Numismatic Notes and Monographs of the Numismatic Society of India 18), (Varanasi, 1980), p. 48.

view that they might represent the names of mint cities,[1] although he admitted that all the known monograms, 'or even half' of them, could not be explained in this manner.[2] Moreover, the number of monograms is too large to be the names of mint cities.[3]

Percy Gardner also regarded the monograms as representing the names of mints.[4] But E J Rapson criticized this view on the ground that, of the two monograms occurring on the overstruck *Kaviśiye-nagara-devatā* coin, none could be resolved to give the letters which go to make the name Kāpiśī.[5] Recently, Michael Mitchinier put forth the suggestion that the various monograms occurring on these coins may be associated with one of the three regions—(i) north of the Hindukush; (ii) between the Hindukush and the river Indus; and (iii) east of the river Indus. But some of the monograms occur on coins discovered in more than one of these regions, to explain which phenomenon, he has had to take recourse to the theory of 'daughter mints'.[6]

---

1 Alexander Cunningham, *Coins of Alexander's Successors in the East*, (reprint, Varanasi, 1970), p. 49.

2 Alexander Cunningham, *Coins of Alexander's Successors in the East*, (reprint, Varanasi, 1970), pp. 51ff.

3 A N Lahiri, *Corpus of Indo-Greek Coins*, (Calcutta, 1965), p. 53.

4 Percy Gardner, *Catalogue of the Coins of the Greek and Scythic Kings of Bactria and India, in the British Museum, London*, (reprint, New Delhi, 1971), p. lvi.

5 E J Rapson, Indian Coins and Seals, Pt 6, *Journal of the Royal Asiatic Society of Great Britain and Ireland*, 1905, pp. 783-814, on p. 788.

6 Michael Mitchiner, *Indo-Greek and Indo-Scythian Coinage* 4, (London, 1975), Appendix 1.

Scholars, like R B Whitehead,[1] Alberto M Simonetta,[2] and A H Dani,[3] have sought to associate the monograms with local magistrates or moneyers or assayers. As regards the continued use of a particular monogram over a long period of time, it has been suggested that such monograms were used, not by individual persons, but by their families.[4] Dani would associate the monograms with hereditary assayers or with families of assayers, who might not have been government officials, but who represented the 'market interests', and tested the coins for the purity of the metal.[5] Tarn also thinks along the same lines,[6] but he also finds the theory of McDowell quite 'attractive', that the monograms 'were at the start moneyers' monograms which became stereotyped to mean certain mints'.[7] Osmund Bopearachchi seems to

1 R B Whitehead, *Pre-Mohammadan Coinage of North-West India*, (Numismatic Notes and Monographs of the American Numismatic Society 13), (New York, 1922), pp. 26-27.

2 Alberto M Simonetta, An Essay on the So-called 'Indo-Greek' Coinage, *East and West* 8, (1957), pp. 44-66, on pp. 55-66.

3 A H Dani, Greek Monograms, in David W MacDowall, Savita Sharma, and Sanjay Garg (ed), *Indian Numismatics, History, Art, and Culture—Essays in the Honour of Dr P L Gupta* 1, (Delhi, 1992), pp. 99-114, on p. 105.

4 See W W Tarn, *The Greeks in Bactria and India*, (reprint, New Delhi, 1980), p. 440; Alberto M Simonetta, An Essay on the So-called 'Indo-Greek' Coinage, *East and West* 8, (1957), pp. 44-66, on pp. 55-66.

5 A H Dani, Greek Monograms, in David W MacDowall, Savita Sharma, and Sanjay Garg (ed), *Indian Numismatics, History, Art, and Culture—Essays in the Honour of Dr P L Gupta* 1, (Delhi, 1992), pp. 99-114, on p. 105.

6 W W Tarn, *The Greeks in Bactria and India*, (reprint, New Delhi, 1980), Appendix 1, pp. 435-441.

7 W W Tarn, *The Greeks in Bactria and India*, (reprint, New Delhi, 1980), p. 439, n. 5.

be inclined to favour, with certain modifications, the view of Bivar,[1] that the monogram forms, apparently forming a homogenous series, might be linked to particular mints, the difference between the various monograms within each series being due to the various *officinae* attached to the same mint.[2] Bopearachchi proposes 36 such monogram series.[3]

Kushāṇa coins also bear a monogram or symbol on the reverse. These symbols are formed by a combination of straight lines, angles, circles and dots (coin no. 53); one symbol is similar to a *nandipada*.[4] A N Lahiri[5] and A H Dani[6] give a list of 441 monograms on Indo-Greek coins, but, according to another estimate, over 550 monograms have so far been reported on Indo-Greek coins, although some readings are believed to be incorrect, and, after eliminating these incorrect readings, the total number of monograms

---

1 A D H Bivar, The Bactra Coinage of Euthydemus and Demetrius, *Numismatic Chronicle*, 1951, pp. 22ff, on pp. 22-23.

2 See Prashant Srivastava, *Encyclopaedia of Indian Coins (Ancient Coins of Northern India, up to* circa *650 AD)* 1, (Delhi, 2012), pp. 262-264.

3 See Prashant Srivastava, *Encyclopaedia of Indian Coins (Ancient Coins of Northern India, up to* circa *650 AD)* 1, (Delhi, 2012), pp. 262-264.

4 See A S Altekar, *The Coinage of the Gupta Empire*, (Corpus of Indian Coins 4), (Varanasi, 1957), pl. XXVII; also S R Goyal, *The Coinage of Ancient India*, (Jodhpur, 1995), p. 260.

5 A N Lahiri, *Corpus of Indo-Greek Coins*, (Calcutta, 1965), plates A-C.

6 A H Dani, Greek Monograms, in David W MacDowall, Savita Sharma, and Sanjay Garg (ed), *Indian Numismatics, History, Art, and Culture—Essays in the Honour of Dr P L Gupta* 1, (Delhi, 1992), pp. 99-114, on pp. 106-114.

on these coins has been reduced to around 250 or 300.[1] R C Senior gives a list of 248 monograms on Śaka-Pahlava coins.[2] However, the number of symbols on Kushāṇa coins does not even reach the figure of ten.[3] Also, each symbol on the Kushāṇa coins seems to be peculiar to a particular king, although there are some rare exceptions to this rule.[4]

The gold issues of the Imperial Guptas bear 'a small geometric type of drawing occurring on the reverse...and consisting of a circle or parallelogram, usually hanging down from a line with a number of prongs or dots above it' (coins no. 54-57).[5] V A Smith refers to them as monograms.[6] Very rarely, the Gupta coins bear two symbols on the reverse,[7]

---

1 See Prashant Srivastava, *Encyclopaedia of Indian Coins (Ancient Coins of Northern India, up to* circa *650 AD)* 1, (Delhi, 2012), pp. 262-264.

2 R C Senior, *Indo-Scythian Coins and History* 1, ((Lancaster, Pennsylvania, London, 2001), p. 207.

3 A S Altekar, *Catalogue of the Gupta Gold Coins in the Bayana Hoard*, (Bombay, 1954), pl. XLVIII.

4 A S Altekar, *Catalogue of the Gupta Gold Coins in the Bayana Hoard*, (Bombay, 1954), p. cxxxii; Bhaskar Chattopadhyay, *The Age of the Kushāṇas—A Numismatic Study*, (Calcutta, 1967), pp. 224-231; S R Goyal, *The Coinage of Ancient India*, (Jodhpur, 1995), p. 260.

5 A S Altekar, *The Coinage of the Gupta Empire*, (Corpus of Indian Coins 4), (Varanasi, 1957), p. 287, and pl. XXVII.

6 V A Smith, *Coins of Ancient India—Catalogue of the Coins in the Indian Museum, Calcutta, including the Cabinet of the Asiatic Society of Bengal* 1, (reprint, Varanasi, 1972), pl. XVIII.

7 A S Altekar, *The Coinage of the Gupta Empire*, (Corpus of Indian Coins 4), (Varanasi, 1957), pl. I. 8; pl. IV. 10; etc.

in which case, the second one is relatively simpler.[1] But the practice of showing a second symbol on the coins was discontinued during or after the reign of Chandragupta II.[2] On certain coins, the symbol is absent altogether, as in the case of the Tiger-slayer type of Samudragupta.[3] The symbols on Imperial Gupta coins have been explained, by various scholars, variously as marks of the mint master,[4] as denoting the mint city,[5] as of religious significance,[6] as auspicious symbols,[7] as denoting the total number of coins of a single type issued in a particular mint operation,[8] or as denoting the date of the issue of a coin.[9] But all these explanations do not appear to be very convincing. Altekar, after examining in detail all these explanations, comes to the conclusion that, most probably, 'early Gupta mint-masters regarded these

---

1 A S Altekar, *The Coinage of the Gupta Empire*, (Corpus of Indian Coins 4), (Varanasi, 1957), p. 288.

2 A S Altekar, *The Coinage of the Gupta Empire*, (Corpus of Indian Coins 4), (Varanasi, 1957), p. 288.

3 A S Altekar, *The Coinage of the Gupta Empire*, (Corpus of Indian Coins 4), (Varanasi, 1957), pl. III. 13-14.

4 A S Altekar, *Catalogue of the Gupta Gold Coins in the Bayana Hoard*, (Bombay, 1954), pp. cxxxiii-cxxxix; S R Goyal, *The Coinage of Ancient India*, (Jodhpur, 1995), p. 355.

5 A S Altekar, *Catalogue of the Gupta Gold Coins in the Bayana Hoard*, (Bombay, 1954), pp. cxxxiii-cxxxix; S R Goyal, *The Coinage of Ancient India*, (Jodhpur, 1995), p. 355.

6 V A Smith, The Coinage of the Early or Imperial Gupta Dynasty of Northern India, *Journal of the Royal Asiatic Society of Great Britain and Ireland*, 1889, pp. 1-41, on p. 33.

7 S R Goyal, *The Coinage of Ancient India*, (Jodhpur, 1995), p. 355.

8 B S Sitholey, Symbols on Gupta Coins, *Journal of the Numismatic Society of India* 11(2), (1949), pp. 111-113, on p. 111.

9 S R Goyal, *The Coinage of Ancient India*, (Jodhpur, 1995), p. 355.

symbols on their prototype as merely decorative elements which they were free to diversify in any artistic way they liked'.[1]

1 A S Altekar, *The Coinage of the Gupta Empire*, (Corpus of Indian Coins 4), (Varanasi, 1957), p. 290.

10

Coin denominations

There are certain coin denominations, which find mention in literature and epigraphs, but their import is not very clear.

Nāṇaka. This seems to have originally denoted the coins of the Kushāṇa ruler, Kanishka I, because of the appearance of the figure of the goddess, *Nana*, on his coins for the first time in India.[1] A commentator on Yājñavalkya explains *nāṇaka* as *Nāṇāṅka ṭaṅka*, that is a coin 'having Nāṇā (*Nana* ?) as... cognisance'.[2] The commentator of the *Mṛichchhakaṭikam* explains it as *Śivāṅka ṭaṅka*,[3] perhaps because of the figure of Śiva appearing on the coins of ıhis ruler.[4] Most of the scholars hold that *nāṇaka* denoted Kushāṇa gold coins. But

---

1 B N Mukherjee, *Nana on Lion—A Study in Kushāṇa Numismatic Art*, (Calcutta, 1969), p. 57.

2 J N Banerjea, Coinage, Chapter XXV, in K A N Sastri (ed), *A Comprehensive History of India* 2, The Mauryas and Sātavāhanas (325 BC - AD 300), (Calcutta, 1957), pp. 777-811, on pp. 795-796.

3 See H M S Sastri and K P Parab (ed), *Mṛichchhakaṭikam*, p. 19n.

4 B N Mukherjee, Impact of the Kushāṇa Coinage on Early Indian Indigenous Coins, in A M Shastri (ed), *Foreign Elements in Indian*

from the *Aṅgavijjā*, which says that a *ṇāṇaka* was much inferior in value to a *kārshāpaṇa*,[1] it appears that *nāṇaka* was a copper coin, and the impression is reinforced by the *Mṛichchhakaṭikam*.[2] Yājñavalkya (*c* 100-300 AD) refers to one who counterfeits coins as *kūṭakṛit-nāṇakasya*, and to coin-examiner as *nāṇaka-parīkshī*.[3] In the *Mṛichchhakaṭikam* occurs the term *nāṇaka-mūśi*, '[one] who robs [people] of *nāṇakas* (= coins or wealth)'.[4] The *Bṛihatkalpasūtrabhāshya* (*c* seventh century AD) refers to coins of gold, silver, and copper as *suvarṇa-nāṇaka*, *rūpamaya-nāṇaka*, and *tāmramaya-nāṇaka*, respectively.[5] From this, it has been inferred that *nāṇaka* seems to have become a generic name for all types of coins.[6]

Indigenous Coins, (Memoirs of the Numismatic Society of India 8), (Varanasi, 1982), pp. 13-26, on p. 25, n. 85.

1 V S Agrawala, Coin Names in the *Aṅgavijjā*, *Journal of the Numismatic Society of India* 19(1), (1957), pp. 20-31, on p. 23.

2 See B N Mukherjee, Impact of the Kushāṇa Coinage on Early Indian Indigenous Coins, in A M Shastri (ed), *Foreign Elements in Indian Indigenous Coins*, (Memoirs of the Numismatic Society of India 8), (Varaṇasi, 1982), pp. 13-26, on p. 21.

3 *Yājñavalkyasmṛiti*, Vyāvahāra-adhyāya, verse 241.

4 *Mṛichchhakaṭikam*, I. 23.

5 Punyavijaya (ed), *Bṛihatkalpasūtrabhāshya* 2, p. 573, *vide* B N Mukherjee, Impact of the Kushāṇa Coinage on Early Indian Indigenous Coins, in A M Shastri (ed), *Foreign Elements in Indian Indigenous Coins*, (Momoirs of the Numismatic Society of India 8), (Varanasi, 1982), pp. 13-26, on p. 21, and n. 83.

6 B N Mukherjee, Impact of the Kushāṇa Coinage on Early Indian Indigenous Coins, in A M Shastri (ed), *Foreign Elements in Indian Indigenous Coins*, (Memoirs of the Numismatic Society of India 8), (Varanasi, 1982), pp. 13-26, on p. 21. See also Chandrashekhar Gupta, Foreign Denominations of Early Indian Coins, in A M Shastri (ed), *Foreign Elements in Indian Indigenous Coins*, (Memoirs of the

Rudradāmaka. This denomination is mentioned in the *Sāratthadīpanī*, the commentary on the *Samantapāsādikā* of Buddhaghosha by Śāriputra. According to C D Chatterjee, it implied the silver coins struck by Rudradāman [I] (*Rudradāmena uppādito*).[1] D C Sircar, however, regards the *rudradāmaka* as the silver coins issued by the Western Kshatrapas in general, and named after Rudradāman I, 'the greatest and most famous of the Śaka rulers of Western India'.[2] According to this commentary, it was three-fourth the value of a *nīla-kahāpaṇa*,[3] the standard silver *kārshāpaṇa* of 32 *rattīs*.[4] From this, it has been inferred that the *rudradāmaka* weighed 24 *rattīs* (or, more probably, 20 *rattīs*).[5] However, in inscriptions, Western Kshatrapa silver coins are often mentioned as *kārshāpaṇa*.[6]

Numismatic Society of India 8), (Varanasi, 1982), pp. 109-123, on pp. 115-116.

1 C D Chatterjee, Some Numismatic Data in Pāli Literature, in B C Law (ed), *Buddhistic Studies* 4, (Calcutta, 1931), pp. 383-452, on pp. 389-395, 419-437.

2 D C Sircar, *Studies in Indian Coins*, (Delhi, 1968), p. 98.

3 C D Chatterjee, Some Numismatic Data in Pāli Literature, in B C Law (ed), *Buddhistic Studies* 4, (Calcutta, 1931), pp. 383-452, on p. 385, extract ii.

4 D C Sircar, *Studies in Indian Coins*, (Delhi, 1968), pp. 99-100.

5 V S Agrawala, Coin Names in the *Aṅgavijjā*, *Journal of the Numismatic Society of India* 19(1), (1957), pp. 20-31, on p. 23; D C Sircar, *Studies in Indian Coins*, (Delhi, 1968), pp. 98.

6 See, for example, the Nasik cave inscription of the time of Nahapāna, years 41, 42, 45, line 5, D C Sircar, *Select Inscriptions bearing on Indian History and Civilization, from 6 century BC to 6 century AD* 1, (3rd ed, Delhi, 1986), p. 166.

Rudradāmakādi. This denomination occurs in the *Samantapāsādikā* of Buddhaghosha, and the *Vinayatthamañjūshā*, the commentary on the *Kaṅkhāvitaraṇī* of Buddhaghosha by Buddhanāga.[1] C D Chatterjee interprets it as silver coins, which have been modelled after the *rudradāmaka*, and issued by the successors of Rudradāman I.[2] D C Sircar, however, objects to this on the ground that all the Western Kshatrapa coins are based on the same weight standard, and it would not have been possible for the common man of the time to distinguish between the coins of the Kārddamaka Kshatrapas from those of the other Śaka rulers of western India.[3] He, himself, regards *rudradāmakādi* as denoting the whole class of silver coins, based on the weight standard of 36 grains, issued by the Western Kshatrapas, as well as the 'non-Śaka silver coins of about the same weight standard such as those of the Sātavāhanas and the Guptas'.[4] However, as stated above, in inscriptions, Western Kshatrapa silver coins are mentioned as *kārshāpaṇa*.[5]

---

1 C D Chatterjee, Some Numismatic Data in Pāli Literature, in B C Law (ed), *Buddhistic Studies* 4, (Calcutta, 1931), pp. 383-452, on p. 392.

2 C D Chatterjee, Some Numismatic Data in Pāli Literature, in B C Law (ed), *Buddhistic Studies* 4, (Calcutta, 1931), pp. 383-452, on p. 392.

3 D C Sircar, *Studies in Indian Coins*, (Delhi, 1968), p. 98.

4 D C Sircar, *Studies in Indian Coins*, (Delhi, 1968), p. 98.

5 See, for example, the Nasik cave inscription of the time of Nahapāna, years 41, 42, 45, line 5, D C Sircar, *Select Inscriptions bearing on Indian History and Civilization, from 6 century BC to 6 century AD* 1, (3rd ed, Delhi, 1986), p. 166.

Muli. This term seems to occur as the name of a class of coins in the Niya Kharoshṭhī documents,[1] from the time of King Pepiye of the Shan Shan kingdom,[2] and by the time of Vashmana, who seems to the third successor of that ruler, it had become the predominant currency in Chinese Turkestan, and might have superseded other coins like the *sadera/satera*, *drakhma/trakhma*, and, perhaps, also *māsha*.[3] It is not certain whether, as a currency, it was of indigenous or foreign origin.[4] Scholars like H W Bailey, however, express doubts regarding *muli* being at all a coin denomination, and feel that it might have been used in the sense of 'price' or 'value' (Sanskrit, *mūlya*) only.[5]

---

1 M Aurel Stein, *Kharoshṭhī Inscriptions Discovered by Sir A Stein in Chinese Turkestan*, 3 vols. Oxford, 1929; T Burrow, *A Translation of the Kharoshṭhī Documents from Chinese Turkestan*, London, 1940.

2 R C Agrawala, Numismatic Data in Niya Kharoshṭhī Documents from Central Asia, *Journal of the Numismatic Society of India* 16(2), (1954), pp. 219-230, on p. 220.

3 R C Agrawala, Numismatic Data in Niya Kharoshṭhī Documents from Central Asia, *Journal of the Numismatic Society of India* 16(2), (1954), pp. 219-230, on p. 221.

4 R C Agrawala, Numismatic Data in Niya Kharoshṭhī Documents from Central Asia, *Journal of the Numismatic Society of India* 16(2), (1954), pp. 219-230, on p. 220.

5 H W Bailey, in a personal note, dated 19 April 1953, to R C Agrawala. See R C Agrawala, Numismatic Data in Niya Kharoshṭhī Documents from Central Asia, *Journal of the Numismatic Society of India* 16(2), (1954), pp. 219-230, on p. 220, n. 5, and p. 223.

11

An illustrative problem of forgery

Unscrupulous persons have been forging coins, with a view to earning money and/or fame. This is not a recent phenomenon, as shown by the discovery of ancient moulds to forge Sātavāhana silver coins. Such forged coins create various kinds of problems for numismatists.

Silver coins of Chandragupta I-Kumāradevī type. The gold coins of this type (coins no. 54-57) were first issued by Chandragupta I, conjointly with Kumāradevī, who was not a mere queen-consort, but a queen-regnant, and the type was the result of a rare political situation, when the queen was co-ruling with her husband. Some scholars would, however, ascribe it, variously, to Samudragupta, or the Lichchhavis, and suggest that the coins were issued to commemorate the marriage of Chandragupta I with Kumāradevī. The obverse of these gold coins shows the king, wearing a long coat and trousers (that is the Kushāṇa type dress) standing left, with a crescent topped standard in his left hand, and offering some object (ring or bangle or *sindūradānī*) to the queen standing to his right. The queen is looking at the object being offered to her by the king. Her left hand hangs down; her right hand is on waist. Sometimes, there is a crescent between the heads of the royal couple. The vertical legend, below the king's arm, reads *Chandra-*, and that outside the standard, *-guptaḥ*. On the left, is the legend, *Śrī-Kumāradevī*, or *Kumāradevī-Śrīḥ*. The reverse has *Siṁhavāhinī Devī*, with a *pāśa* in her right hand, and a *cornucopiae* in her left hand. The legend reads *Lichchhavayaḥ*. New dimension is added to the issue by the discovery of some silver coins of the Chandragupta I-Kumāradevī type. A L Srivastava was, probably, the first scholar to bring a silver coin of this type to the notice of the scholarly world,[1] and he reports that this coin is similar to the gold coins of this type is almost every respect. Later on, other silver coins of this type were published by Y B Singh,[2] O P Singh,[3] and B R Mani.[4]

B R Mani points out that there are three differences between the silver coins examined by him, and the gold coins of the Chandragupta I-Kumāradevī type. First, the name of Chandragupta I is written on the gold pieces as *Chandra*, while it occurs as *Chaṁdra* on the silver pieces. Secondly, the crescent, seen between the heads of Chandragupta I and

---

1 A L Srivastava, A Silver Coin of Chandragupta-Kumāradevī Type, *Journal of the Numismatic Society of India* 37, (1975), pp. 83-84.

2 Y B Singh, Some Recently Found Silver Coins of the Imperial Guptas, *Journal of the Numismatic Society of India* 41, (1979), pp. 47-50.

3 O P Singh, A Note on Silver Coin of Chandragupta I and Kumāradevī, *Journal of the Numismatic Society of India* 44, (1982), pp. 48-51, on p. 48, pl. IV. 10.

4 B R Mani, New Evidence Concerning Gold Prototype Silver Coins of the Gupta Emperors, *Journal of the Numismatic Society of India* 43(2), (1981), pp. 54-59, on p. 56, pl. II. 4.

Kumāradevī on the gold coins, is absent on the silver coins.[1] And last, the name of Kumāradevī occurs on the silver pieces, without the honorific title of *śrī*.[2] A fourth difference is that, on the silver pieces, between the legs of the king on the obverse, there appears a Brāhmī letter, *la*.[3] As the occurrence of Brāhmī letters on the obverse of the coins is a feature of the Kushāṇa coinage, the silver coins of the Chandragupta I-Kumāradevī type, which bear the Brāhmī letter, *la*, on the obverse, have been placed chronologically earlier than the gold coins of this type, on which no such solitary Brāhmī letters occur in the field.[4]

All this leads to an intriguing question—When silver is much less valuable than gold, why have the gold coins of the Chandragupta I-Kumāradevī been found in relatively larger numbers, and also in coin hoards, while the silver coins are very rare, and are not definitely known to have come from any hoards ? Besides, it is known that symbols occur only on the gold coins of the Imperial Guptas, and not

---

1 On the coin published by O P Singh, this crescent is present between the heads of the royal couple. See O P Singh, A Note on Silver Coin of Chandragupta I and Kumāradevī, *Journal of the Numismatic Society of India* 44, (1982), pp. 48-51, on p. 48, pl. IV. 10.

2 B R Mani, New Evidence Concerning Gold Prototype Silver Coins of the Gupta Emperors, *Journal of the Numismatic Society of India* 43(2), (1981), pp. 54-59, on pp. 58-59.

3 This has been pointed out by O P Singh, A Note on Silver Coin of Chandragupta I and Kumāradevī, *Journal of the Numismatic Society of India* 44, (1982), pp. 48-51, on p. 48.

4 See O P Singh, A Note on Silver Coin of Chandragupta I and Kumāradevī, *Journal of the Numismatic Society of India* 44, (1982), pp. 48-51, on p. 51, where he says, 'Non-occurrence of Brāhmī letters on the gold coins suggests these pieces were issued after the silver currency.'

on their silver and copper issues.[1] Still, the silver coins of the Chandragupta I-Kumāradevī type mostly bear symbols. This leads to another intriguing question—If the silver issues of the first Gupta emperor bear symbols, why are such symbols conspicuous by their absence on the silver coins of the subsequent Gupta emperors ?

Y B Singh regards the silver coin published by him as an example of mint-testing, due to the presence of traces of gold in the coin.[2] But one is at a loss to understand as to why silver had to be used in the royal mint for testing the dies of a gold coin. B N Mukherjee has expressed grave doubts, regarding the genuineness of the silver coins of the Chandragupta I-Kumāradevī type.[3] He says that none of these silver pieces has been recovered from an excavation, or from a coin hoard. He also says that a silver coin of this type, examined by him, appears to be a cast piece, while genuine Gupta coins appear to be die-struck. As such, he regards that silver coin of the Chandragupta I-Kumāradevī type, examined by him, as a forgery, and concludes : 'All these considerations do not allow us to accept (in the present state of our knowledge) these silver pieces as products of a Gupta mint.'[4]

---

1 A S Altekar, *The Coinage of the Gupta Empire*, (Corpus of Indian Coins 4), (Varanasi, 1957), p. 287.

2 Y B Singh, Some Recently Found Silver Coins of the Imperial Guptas, *Journal of the Numismatic Society of India* 41, (1979), pp. 47-50, on p. 47.

3 B N Mukherjee, *Art in Gupta and Post-Gupta Coinages*, (Lucknow, 1985), p. 16.

4 B N Mukherjee, *Art in Gupta and Post-Gupta Coinages*, (Lucknow, 1985), p. 30, n. 28.

Select Bibliography

Agrawal, Ashvini 1989. *Rise and Fall of the Imperial Guptas*. Delhi.

Agrawala, R C 1952. Numismatic Data in the Kharoshṭhī Documents from Chinese Turkestan. *Journal of the Numismatic Society of India* 14, pp. 103-106.

Agrawala, R C 1954. Numismatic Data in the Niya Kharoshṭhī Documents from Central Asia. *Journal of the Numismatic Society of India* 16(2), pp. 219-230.

Agrawala, R C 1954. Coins, Weights and Measures in the Bakhshali Manuscript. *Journal of the Numismatic Society of India* 16(2), pp. 231-235.

Agrawala, V S 1950. Presidential Address at the Nagpur Session of the Numismatic Society of India (Hindi). *Journal of the Numismatic Society of India* 12(2), pp. 188-205.

Agrawala, V S 1953. Ancient Coins as known to Pāṇini. *Journal of the Numismatic Society of India* 15(1), pp. 27-41.

Agrawala, V S 1957. Coin Names in the *Aṅgavijjā*. *Journal of the Numismatic Society of India* 19(1), pp. 20-31.

Allan, John 1914. *Catalogue of the Coins of the Gupta Dynasties, and of Śaśāṅka, King of Gauḍa, in the British Museum, London*. London.

Allan, John 1936. *Catalogue of the Coins of Ancient India, in the British Museum, London*. London.

Altekar, A S 1947. Identity of Kāchagupta. *Journal of the Numismatic Society of India* 9(2), pp. 131-136.

Altekar, A S 1953. Origin and Early History of Coinage in Ancient India. *Journal of the Numismatic Society of India* 15(1), pp. 1-26.

Altekar, A S 1954. *Catalogue of the Gupta Gold Coins in the Bayana Hoard*. Bombay.

Altekar, A S 1957. *The Coinage of the Gupta Empire*. Corpus of Indian Coins, IV. Varanasi.

Altekar, A S 1986. The Coinage. Chapter XV, in R C Majumdar and A S Altekar (ed), *The Vākāṭaka-Gupta Age (c 200-550 AD)*. A New History of the Indian People 6, (Delhi, 1986), pp. 295-308.

Audouin, R, and P Bernard 1973. *Trésor de Monnaies Indiennes et Indo-Grecques d'Aï Khanoum* (Afghanistan). *Revue Numismatique*, pp. 238-289.

Bachhofer, L 1941. On Greeks and Śakas in India. *Journal of the American Oriental Society*, pp. 223ff.

Bajpai, K D 1976. *Indian Numismatic Studies*. New Delhi.

Bajpai, K D 1989. Bodhisattva and Buddha : The Early Iconic Forms. *Buddhist Iconography* (Sambhota Series 2, Tibet House, New Delhi), pp. 60-68.

Bajpai, K D 1991. Ancient Indian Numismatics : Symbology and the Decorative Aspect. *Numismatic Studies* 1, pp. 111-120.

Banerjea, J N 1950. The Obverse Device of Some *Decadrachms* with Alexandrian Association. *Journal of the Numismatic Society of India* 12(2), pp. 118-120.

Banerjea, J N 1968. *Religion in Art and Archaeology*. R K Mookerji Endowment Lectures, University of Lucknow, 1961-1962. Lucknow.

Banerjea, J N 2002. *The Development of Hindu Iconography*. 5th ed, New Delhi.

Banerji, R D 1933. *The Age of the Imperial Guptas*. Manindra Chandra Nandi Lectures, 1924, revised by the author in 1929-1930. Varanasi.

Barton, George A 1990. *The Religions of the World*. Reprint, New Delhi.

Basham, A L 1953. A New Study of the Śaka-Kuṣāṇa Period (review of J E van Lohuizen-de Leeuw, *The "Scythian" Period*). *Bulletin of the School of Oriental and African Studies* 15, pp. 80-97.

Bayer, T S 1738. *Historia Regni Graecorum Bactriani*. St Petersbourg.

Beckert, Heinz 1995. *When Did Buddha Live. The Controversy of the Dating of the Historical Buddha*. (English translation of *Die Datierung des Historischen Buddha*, 2 vols. Göttingen, 1991-1992). Delhi.

Bhandarkar, D R 1981. *Corpus Inscriptionum Indicarum* 3. Inscriptions of the Early Gupta Kings. Ed by B Ch Chhabra and G S Gai. New Delhi.

Bhandarkar, D R 1984. *Carmichael Lectures in Ancient Indian Numismatics*. Reprint, Patna.

Bhandarkar, R G 1928. *Vaishṇavism, Śaivism and Some Minor Religious Systems*. Poona.

Bhatia, Pratipal 1989. Coins. A Ghosh (ed), *An Encyclopaedia of Indian Archaeology* 1 (New Delhi, 1989), pp. 10-14.

Bhattacharji, Sukumari 1970. *The Indian Theogony*. Cambridge.

Bhattacharya, Sibesh 1992. Ghaṭotkacha : The King Kācha of Coins. B Ch Chhabra, P K Agrawala, Ashvini Agrawal, and Shankar Goyal (ed), *Reappraising Gupta History for S R Goyal*, (New Delhi, 1992), pp. 77-82.

Bhattasali, N K 1923. Notes on Gupta and Later Gupta Coinages. *Journal of the Asiatic Society of Bengal, Numismatic Supplement* 37, pp. 54-64.

Bopearachchi, Osmund 1993. *Indo-Greek, Indo-Scythian and Indo-Parthian Coins in the Smithsonian Institution*. Smithsonian Institution, Washington D C.

Bopearachchi, Osmund 1994. Recent Discoveries : Hoards and Finds of Ancient Coins from Afghanistan and Pakistan. *Yavanika* (Journal of the Indian Society for Greek and Roman Studies) 4, pp. 3-30.

Bopearachchi, Osmund 2004. Two Rare Pre-Kushan Coins. *Newsletter of the Oriental Numismatic Society* 178, pp. 18-20.

Bopearachchi, Osmund, and Wilfried Pieper 1998. *Ancient Indian Coins*. Brepols, Turnhout.

Bopearachchi, Osmund, and A U Rahman 1995. *Pre-Kushāṇa Coins in Pakistan*. Islamabad.

Brown, C J 1973. *The Coin of India*. Reprint, Varanasi.

Bühler, Georg 2001. *The Laws of Manu*. Sacred Books of the East 25. Reprint, Delhi.

Burn, Richard 1945. Coinage Bearing the Names of Indian Queens. *Journal of the Numismatic Society of India* 7, pp. 69-77.

Burns, Craig Alden, and Shafqat Mirza 1990. Topi Hoard of Kushāṇa Dīnāras. *Numismatic Digest* 14, pp. 16-21.

Burrow, T 1940. *A Translation of the Kharoshṭhī Documents from Chinese Turkestan*. London.

Chakrabortty, S K 1931. *A Study of Ancient Indian Numismatics* (Indigenous System) from the Earliest Times to the Rise of the Imperial Guptas. Mymensingh.

Chamberlain, C C 1960. *Guide to Numismatics*. London.

Chatterjee, C D 1931. Some Numismatic Data in Pāli Literature. B C Law (ed), *Buddhistic Studies* 4 (Calcutta), pp. 383ff.

Chatterjee, C D 1933. Some Numismatic Terms in Pāli Texts. *Journal of the U P Historical Society* 6(1), pp. 156-173.

Chattopadhyay, Bhaskar 1967. *The Age of the Kushāṇas—A Numismatic Study*. Calcutta.

Chattopadhyay, Bhaskar 1977. *Coins and Icons—A Study of Myths and Symbols in Indian Numismatic Art*. Calcutta.

Chattopadhyaya, Sudhakar 1955. *The Śakas in India*. Santiniketan.

Chattopadhyaya, Sudhakar 1958. *Early History of North India*. Calcutta.

Chhabra, B Ch 1986. *Catalogue of the Gupta Gold Coins of the Bayana Hoard in the National Museum, New Delhi*. New Delhi.

Coomaraswamy, A K 2001. *Yakṣas*, 2 parts. Reprint, New Delhi.

Coomaraswamy, A K 2003. *Buddha and the Gospel of Buddhism*. Reprint, New Delhi.

Cowell, E B (ed) 2005. *The Jātaka or Stories of the Buddha's Former Births*. Translated from the Pāli by various hands, 6 vols. Reprint, Delhi.

Cribb, Joe 1980. Kaniṣka's Buddha Coins—The Official Iconography of Śākyamuni and Maitreya. *Journal of the International Association of Buddhist Studies* 3(2), pp. 79-88, and plates.

Cribb, Joe 1985. Indian's Earliest Coins ? *Coins Haords* 7, pp. 278-281.

Cribb, Joe 1999-2000. Kanishka's Buddha Image Coins Revisited. *Silk Road Art and Archaeology* 6, pp. 151-189.

Cribb, Joe 2005. *The Indian Coinage Tradition : Origins, Continuity and Change*. Nashik.

Cribb, Joe, and Nicholas Sims-Williams 1995-1996. A New Bactrian Inscription of Kanishka the Great. *Silk Road Art and Archaeology* 4, The Institute of Silk Road Studies, Kamakura, pp. 75-142.

Cunningham, Alexander 1962. *Later Indo-Scythians*. Reprinted from *Numismatic Chronicle* 1893-1895. Indian reprint, Varanasi.

Cunningham, Alexander 1967. *Coins of Mediaeval India.* Reprint, Delhi.

Cunningham, Alexander 1970. *Coins of Alexander's Successors in the* East. Reprint, Varanasi.

Cunningham, Alexander 1971. *Coins of the Indo-Scythians, Sakas, Kushans.* Reprinted from *Numismatic Chronicle* 1888-1892. Indian reprint, Varanasi.

Cunningham, Alexander 1971. *Coins of Ancient India.* Reprint, Varanasi.

Dani, A H 1992. Greek Monograms. D W Macdowall, Savita Sharma, and Sanjay Garg (ed), *Indian Numismatics, History, Art, and Culture* (Essays in the Honour of Dr P L Gupta), (Delhi, 1992), pp. 99-114.

Dani, A H 1997. *Indian Palaeography.* Reprint, New Delhi.

Darmesteter, J 1974. *The Zend-Avesta*, 3 parts. Sacred Books of the East 4, 23, 31. Reprint, Delhi.

Dasgupta, C C 1958. *The Development of the Kharoṣṭhī Script.* Calcutta.

Dasgupta, K K 1974. *A Tribal History of Ancient India—A Numismatic Approach.* Calcutta.

Davary, G Djelani, and Helmut Humbach 1976. *Die Baktrische Inschrift IDN 1 von Dasht-e Nāwūr (Afghanistan). Akademie der Wissenschaften und der Literatur, Abhandlungen der Geistes- und Sozialwissenschaftlichen Klasse*, Jahrgang 1976, Nr. 1 (Wiesbaden), pp. 3-21.

Decourdemanche, J-A 1912. *Note sur Les Anciennes Monnaies de L'Inde Dites 'Punch-Marked' Coins et sur Le Système de Manou. Journal Asiatique* January-February 1912, pp. 117-132.

Dhavalikar, M K 1975. The Beginning of Coinage in India. *World Archaeology* 6(3), (London), pp. 330-338.

Diringer, David 2005. *The Alphabet : A Key to the History of Mankind*. Reprint, New Delhi.

Dobbins, K W 1973. *Śaka-Pahlava Coinage*. Memoirs of the Numismatic Society of India 5. Varanasi.

Dobbins, K W 1980. *A Schema of Indo-Baktrian Coinage*. Numismatic Notes and Monographs (Numismatic Society of India) 18. Varanasi.

Durr, Niklaus 1978. New Porus Commemoratives. Translated from the original Swiss by Angelika Ilsch. *Numismatic Digest* 2(1), pp. 4-6, and figures on pp. 8-9.

Fleet, J F 1888. *Corpus Inscriptionum Indicarum* 3. Inscriptions of the Early Gupta Kings and their Successors. Calcutta.

Foss, Michael 1995. *Gods and Heroes : The Story of Greek Mythology*. London.

Foucher, Alfred 2003. *The Life of the Buddha, according to the Ancient Texts and Monuments of India*. Reprint, New Delhi.

Frey, A R 1973. *Dictionary of Numismatic Names*. Reprint, London.

Fussman, G 1974. *Documents Épigraphiques Kouchans, "I. –Inscriptions et Antiquités du Dašt-e Nāwur". Bulletin de l'Ecole Francaise d'Extreme-Orient* 61, pp. 2-50.

Gardner, Percy 1878. *Catalogue of the Coins of the Seleukid Kings, in the British Museum, London*. London.

Gardner, Percy 1887. New Greek Coins of Bactria and India. *Numismatic Chronicle*, pp. 177-181.

Gardner, Percy 1918. *A History of Ancient Coinage (700 BC – 300 BC)*. Oxford.

Gardner, Percy 1971. *Catalogue of the Coins of the Greek and Scythic Kings of Bactria and India, in the British Museum, London*. Indian Reprint, New Delhi.

Ghirshman, Roman 1948. *Begram. Mémoires de la Délégation Archéologique Française en Afghanistan* 13. Cairo.

Ghosh, A (ed) 1989. *An Encyclopaedia of Indian Archaeology*, 2 vols. New Delhi.

Goyal, S R 1984. *A Religious History of Ancient India* 1. Meerut.

Goyal, S R 1986. *A Religious History of Ancient India* 2. Meerut.

Goyal. S R 1994. *Indigenous Coins of Early India*. Jodhpur.

Goyal, S R 1995. *The Dynastic Coins of Ancient India*. Jodhpur.

Goyal, S R 1995. *The Coinage of Ancient India*. Jodhpur.

Goyal, S R 2005. *The Imperial Guptas*. Jodhpur.

Graves, Robert 1955. *The Greek Myths*, 2 vols. Penguin.

Graves, Robert 1960. *Larousse Encyclopaedia of Mythology*. London.

Gupta, C S 1982. Foreign Denominations of Early Indian Coins. A M Shastri (ed), *Foreign Elements in Indian Indigenous Coins*. Memoirs of the Numismatic Society of India 8, (Varanasi, 1982), pp. 109-123.

Gupta, P L 1978. Editor's note on Niklaus Durr, New Porus Commemoratives. *Numismatic Digest* 2(1), pp. 6-7, and figures on pp. 8-9.

Gupta, P L 1998. *The Imperial Guptas* 1. Varanasi.

Gupta, P L 2004. *Coins*. Reprint, NBT, New Delhi.

Gupta, P L, and Terry Hardaker 1985. *Ancient Indian Silver Punch-marked Coins of the Magadha-Maurya Kārshāpaṇa Series*. Nasik.

Handa, Devendra 2005-2006. Huvishka's Buddha Image Gold Coin. *Numismatic Digest* 29-30, pp. 53-58.

Handa, Devendra 2007. *Tribal Coins of Ancient India*. New Delhi.

Handa, Devendra 2007. *Coins and Temples : Numismatic Evidence on the Evolution of Temple Architecture*. Bombay.

Haughton, H L 1946. Notes on Greek and Kushan Coins from the North-West Frontier of India : (a) The Bajaur Hoard of 1942; (b) Some Rare Copper Coins from the North-West Frontier of India. *Numismatic Chronicle*, pp. 141-145.

Head, Barclay V 1911. *Historia Numorum*. London.

Head, Barclay V 1932. *A Guide to the Principal Coins of the Greeks*. London.

Herzfeld, Ernst 1932. *Sakastan*. Berlin.

Hopkins, E W 1902. *Religions of India*. London.

Hopkins, E W 1915. *Epic Mythology*. Strassburg.

Huntington, J C 1993. A Re-examination of a Kanishka Period Tetradrachm Coin Type with an Image of Metrago/Maitreya on the Reverse (Göbl 793. 1) and a Brief Notice on the Importance of the Inscription Relative to Bactro-Gandhāran Buddhist Iconography of the Period. *The Journal of the International Association of Buddhist Studies* 16(2), pp. 355-374.

Iyengar, T R 2003. *Dictionary of Hindu Gods and Goddesses*. New Delhi.

Jayaswal, K P 1920. The Statue of Wema Kadphises and Kushan Chronology. *Journal of the Bihar and Orissa Research Society* 6, pp. 12-22.

Jayaswal, K P 1933. *History of India, 150 AD – 350 AD*. Lahore.

Jenkins, G K 1955. Indo-Scythic Mints. *Journal of the Numismatic Society of India* 17(2), pp. 1ff.

Jenkins, G K, and A K Narain 1957. *The Coin-types of the Śaka-Pahlava Kings of India*. Numismatic Notes and Monographs (Numismatic Society of India) 4. Varanasi.

Junge, Ewald 1984. *World Coin Encyclopaedia*. London.

Kangle, R P 2000. *The Kauṭilīya Arthaśāstra*, 3 parts. Reprint, Delhi.

Kerényi, C 1951. *The Gods of the Greeks*. Translated from the original German text by Norman Cameron. London, New York.

Konow, Sten 1929. *Corpus Inscriptionum Indicarum*, 2(1). Kharoshṭhī Inscriptions with the Exceptions of those of Aśoka. Calcutta.

Konow, Sten 1933. Notes on Indo-Scythian Chronology. *Journal of Indian History* 12, pp. 1-46.

Kosambi, D D 1992. *Indian Numismatics*. Reprint, New Delhi.

Lahiri, A N 1965. *Corpus of Indo-Greek Coins*. Calcutta.

Lahiri, A N 1971. Early Indigenous Coins of Northern India. D C Sircar (ed), *Early Indian Indigenous Coins*, (Calcutta, 1971), pp. 48-77.

Lahiri, A N 1973. Archaic Coins from Northern India. *Journal of the Numismatic Society of India* 35, pp. 1-38.

Lahiri, A N 1977. The So-called Joint Coins of the Indo-Greeks. *Journal of the Numismatic Society of India* 39, pp. 69-76.

Lahiri, Bela 1974. *Indigenous States of Northern India (*circa *200 BC to 320 AD)*. Calcutta.

Lahiri, Bela 1976. India's Earliest Inscribed Coins : The City Issues. *Journal of the Numismatic Society of India* 38(2), pp. 35-54.

van Lohuizen-de Leeuw, J E 1949. *The "Scythian" Period: An Approach to the History, Art, Epigraphy and Palaeography of North India from the 1st century BC to the 3rd century AD*. Leiden.

MacDonald, D, and R C Senior 1998. *The Decline of the Indo-Greeks—A Re-appraisal of the Chronology from the Time of Menander to that of Azes*. Hellenic Numismatic Society, Monograph Series 2.

Macdonald, George 1987. Ancient Greek (Athenian and Macedonian) Coins in India. Appendix to Chapter XV, in E J Rapson (ed), *The Cambridge History of India* 1, (reprint, New Delhi, 1987), pp. 346-350.

Macdonald, George 1987. The Hellenic Kingdoms of Syria, Bactria, and Parthia. Chapter XVII, in E J Rapson (ed), *The Cambridge History of India* 1, (reprint, New Delhi, 1987), pp. 384-419.

Macdonell, A A 1897. *Vedic Mythology*. Strassbourg.

MacDowall, D W 1968. *Soter Megas*, the King of Kings, the Kushāṇa. *Journal of the Numismatic Society of India* 30, pp. 28-48.

MacDowall, D W 2002. The Rabatak Inscription and the Nameless Kushan King, in *Cairo to Kabul : Afghan and Islamic Studies Presented to Ralph Pinder-Wilson* (London), pp. 163-169.

Maity, S K 1970. *The Economic Life of Northern India, in the Gupta Period (*circa *AD 300 - 550)*. 2nd ed, Delhi.

Maity, S K 1970. *Early Indian Coins and Currency System*. New Delhi.

Majumdar, N G 1928-1929. Notes on the Coins of Azes. *Archaeological Survey of India—Annual Review* 1928-1929, pp. 169-174.

Majumdar, R C 1988. The Disintegration of the Empire. Chapter V, in R C Majmudar, A D Pusalker, and A K Majumdar (ed), *The Classical Age*. The History and Culture of the Indian People 3, (Bombay, 1988), pp. 33-41.

Majumdar, R C, A D Pusalker, and A K Majumdar (ed) 1980. *The Age of Imperial Unity*. The History and Culture of the Indian People 2. Bombay.

Majumdar, R C, A D Pusalker, and A K Majumdar (ed) 1988. *The Classical Age*. The History and Culture of the Indian People 3. Bombay.

Majumdar, R C, and A S Altekar (ed) 1986. *The Vākāṭaka-Gupta Age (c 200 – 550 AD)*. A New History of the Indian People 6. Delhi.

Majumdar, R C, and K K Dasgupta (ed) 1981. *A Comprehensive History of India (AD 300 – 985)* 3(1). New Delhi.

Mani, B R 1981. New Evidence Concerning Gold Prototype Silver Coins of the Gupta Emperors. *Journal of the Numismatic Society of India* 43(2), pp. 54-59.

Marshall, J H 1947. Greeks and Śakas in India. *Journal of the Royal Asiatic Society of Great Britain and Ireland*, pp. 3ff.

Marshall, J H 1960. *The Buddhist Art of Gandhāra*. Memoirs of the Department of Archaeology in Pakistan 1. Cambridge.

Marshall, J H 1975. *Taxila*, 3 vols. Indian Reprint, Delhi.

McCrindle, J W 1896. *Invasion of India by Alexander the Great, as described by Arrian, Q Curtius, Diodoros, Plutarch, and Justin*. New edition, Westminster.

McCrindle, J W 1901. *Ancient India as described in Classical Literature*. Westminster.

Mirashi, V V 1982. *Sātavāhanoṁ aura Paśchimī Kshatrapoṁ kā Itihāsa aura Abhilekha* (Hindi). Lucknow.

Mitchiner, Michael 1973. *The Origins of Indian Coinage*. London.

Mitchiner, Michael 1975-1976. *Indo-Greek and Indo-Scythian Coinage*, 9 vols. London.

Mitchiner, Michael 1978. *Oriental Coins and their Values* 2 : *The Ancient and Classical World*. London.

Mitchiner, Michael 2001-2002. The Kushan King, Vima Takshuma, Son of Kujula Kadphises : A Discussion of his Name. *Numismatic Digest* 25-26, pp. 43-50.

von Mitterwallner, Gritli 1986. *Kuṣāṇa Coins and Kuṣāṇa Sculptures from Mathurā*. Mathura.

Monier-Williams, Monier 2005. *A Sanskrit-English Dictionary*. Reprint, Delhi.

Mookerji, R K 1973. *The Gupta Empire*. 5th ed, Delhi.

Mukherjee, B N 1967. *The Kushāṇa Genealogy*. Studies in Kushāṇa Genealogy and Chronology 1. Calcutta.

Mukherjee, B N 1969. *An Agrippan Source—A Study in Indo-Parthian History*. Calcutta.

Mukherjee, B N 1982. Numismatic Art. Appendix to Chapter XXXV, in R C Majumdar and K K Dasgupta (ed), *A Comprehensive History of India (AD 300 – 985)* 3(2), (New Delhi, 1982), pp. 1415-1433.

Mukherjee, B N 1987. Amitābha on Kushāṇa Coins. *Journal of the Numismatic Society of India* 49, pp. 44-45, and plate.

Mukherjee, B N 1995. The Great Kushāṇa Testament. *Indian Museum Bulletin* 30. Calcutta.

Mukherjee, B N 1997-1998. Vima Taktu, An Alleged Kushana King. *Numismatic Digest* 21-22, pp. 5-10.

Narain, A K 1955. *The Coin-types of the Indo-Greek Kings*. Numismatic Notes and Monographs (Numismatic Society of India) 1. Bombay.

Narain, A K 1957. *The Indo-Greeks*. Oxford.

Newell, E T 1938. *The Coinage of the Eastern Selecid Mints*. Numismatic Sudies 1. New York.

Newell, E T 1941. *The Coinage of the Western Seleucid Mints*. Numismatic Studies 4. New York.

Noss, John B 1949. *Man's Religions*. (Macmillan) New York.

Oikonomides, A L N 1973. Soter the Great—The Last of the Indo-Greek Kings. *Journal of the Numismatic Society of India* 35, pp. 82-89.

Pandey, D B 1971. The Hydaspese-Battle Commemorative Medal of Alexander the Great—A Fresh Approach. *Journal of the Numismatic Society of India* 33(2), pp. 1-7.

Pandey, Rajbali 1953. *Indian Palaeography*. Varanasi.

Pinsent, John 1969. *The Greek Mythology*. London.

Prinsep, James 1858. *Essays on Indian Antiquities, Historic, Numismatic, and Palaeographic*. Edited by E Thomas, 2 vols. London.

Puri, B N 1965. *Indian under the Kushāṇas*. Bombay.

Rajgor, Dilip 2001. *Punch-marked Coins of Early Historic India*. San Jose (California), USA.

Rapson, E J 1897. *Indian Coins*. Strassburg.

Rapson, E J 1914. *Ancient India, from the Earliest Times to the First Century AD*. London.

Rapson, E J 1975. *Catalogue of the Coins of the Andhra Dynasty, the Western Kṣatrapas, the Traikūṭaka Dynasty, and the "Bodhi" Dynasty, in the British Museum, London*. Indian reprint, New Delhi.

Rapson, E J (ed) 1987. *The Cambridge History of India* 1. Indian reprint, Delhi.

Rawlinson, H G 1912. *Bactria, the History of a Forgotten Empire*. London.

Rawlinson, H G 1916. *Intercourse between India and the Western World*. Cambridge.

Raychaudhuri, H C 1972. *Political History of Ancient India*, from the Accession of Parīkshita to the Extinction of the Gupta Dynasty. 7th ed, Calcutta.

le Rider, G 1967. *Monnaise de Taxila et d'Arachosie, Une Nouvelle Reine de Taxila. Revue des Études Grecques* 80, pp. 331-342.

Rose, H J 1958. *A Handbook of Greek Mythology, including its Extension to Rome*. London.

Rosenfeld, J M 1967. *The Dynastic Arts of the Kushans*. University of California Press.

Sahai, Bhagwant 1975. *The Iconography of Some Minor Hindu and Buddhist Deities*. Delhi.

von Sallet, A 1883. *Die Nachfolger Alexanders des Grossen in Bactrien und Indien*. Berlin.

Salomon, Richard 1982. The 'Avaca' Inscription and the Origin of the Vikrama Era. *Journal of the American Oriental Society* 102(1), pp. 59-68.

Salomon, Richard 1996. An Inscribed Silver Buddhist Reliquary of the Time of King Kharaosta and Prince Indravarman. *Journal of the American Oriental Society* 116(3), pp. 418-452.

Salomon, Richard 1998. *Indian Epigraphy*. New Delhi.

Sastri, K A N (ed) 1957. *A Comprehensive History of India* 2. Indian History Congress. Place of publication, not mentioned.

Satya Shrava 1981. *The Śakas in India*. New Delhi.

Satya Shrava 1985. *The Kushāṇa Numismatics*. New Delhi.

Senior, R C 1996. The Apracharajas and their Coinage. *Numismatic Digest* 20, pp. 33-40.

Senior, R C 2001. *Indo-Scythian Coins and History*, 3 vols. Lancaster, Pennsylvania, London.

Shastri, A M (ed) 1976. *Coins and Early Indian Economy*. Memoirs of the Numismatic Society of India 6. Varanasi.

Shastri, A M (ed) 1982. *Foreign Elements in Indian Indigenous Coins*. Memoirs of the Numismatic Society of India 8. Varanasi.

Simonetta, Alberto M 1957. An Essay on the So-called 'Indo-Greek' Coinage. *East and West* 8, pp. 44-66.

Simonetta, Alberto M 1958. A New Essay on the Indo-Greeks, the Śakas and the Pahlavas. *East and West* 9, pp. 154-183.

Sims-Williams, Nicholas, and Joe Cribb 1995-1996. See under Cribb, Joe, and Nicholas Sims-Wolliams 1995-1996.

Singh, Y B 1979. Some Recently found Silver Coins of the Imperial Guptas. *Journal of the Numismatic Society of India* 41, pp. 47-50.

Sircar, D C 1966. *Indian Epigraphical Glossary*. Delhi.

Sircar, D C 1968. *Studies in Indian Coins*. Delhi.

Sircar, D C 1971. *Studies in the Religious Life of Ancient and Mediaeval India*. Delhi.

Sircar, D C 1976. Some Problems of Early Indian History. *Journal of the Royal Asiatic Society of Great Britain and Ireland*, pp. 130-135.

Sircar, D C 1980. The Yavanas. Chapter VII, in R C Majumdar, A D Pusalker, and A K Majumdar (ed), *The Age of Imperial Unity*. The History and Culture of the Indian People 2, (Bombay, 1980), pp. 101-119.

Sircar, D C 1980. The Śakas and the Pahlavas. Chapter VIII, in R C Majumdar, A D Pusalker, and A K Majumdar (ed), *The Age of Imperial Unity*. The History and Culture of the Indian People 2, (Bombay, 1980), pp. 120-135.

Sircar, D C 1980. The Kushāṇas. Chapter IX, in R C Majumdar, A D Pusalker, and A K Majumdar (ed), *The Age of Imperial Unity*. The History and Culture of the Indian People 2, (Bombay, 1980), pp. 136-153.

Sircar, D C 1986. *Select Inscriptions bearing on Indian History and Civilization, from 6 century BC to 6 century AD*. 3rd ed, Delhi.

Sircar, D C (ed) 1970. *Early Indian Indigenous Coins*. Calcutta.

Smith, V A 1889. The Coinage of the Early or Imperial Guptas. *Journal of the Royal Asiatic Society of Great Britain and Ireland*, pp. 1-41.

Smith, V A 1893. Observations on Gupta Coinage. *Journal of the Royal Asiatic Society of Great Britain and Ireland*, pp. 17-148.

Smith, V A 1972. *Coins of Ancient India—Catalogue of the Coins in the Indian Museum, Calcutta, including the Cabinet of the Asiatic Society of Bengal* 1. Reprint, Varanasi.

Smith, V A 1999. *The Early History of India*. Third revised and enlarged edition. Reprint, New Delhi.

Srivastava, A L 1975. A Silver Coin of Chandragupta-Kumāradevī Type. *Journal of the Numismatic Society of India* 37, pp. 83-84.

Srivastava, Prashant 1990. *Joint Coin-types of Ancient India.* Numismatic Notes and Monographs (The Numismatic Society of India) 22. Varanasi.

Srivastava, Prashant 1990. Some Observations on the Hermaios-Kalliope Type. *Journal of the Numismatic Society of India* 52, pp. 45-47.

Srivastava, Prashant 1993. On the Identification of the 'Female Between Vines' on the Poseidon Type of Coins. *Journal of the Numismatic Society of India* 55, pp. 112-113.

Srivastava, Prashant 1996. *Aspects of Ancient Indian Numismatics*. Delhi.

Srivastava, Prashant 1998. On the Rarity of Busts and of Realistic Portraiture on Indigenous Indian Coins. *Pañchāla* 10, pp. 131-134.

Srivastava, Prashant 2000-2001. The Beginning of Legends on Ancient Indian Coins. *Purāvṛitta* (Journal of the Department of Ancient Indian History and Archaeology, University of Lucknow) 1, pp. 215-220.

Srivastava, Prashant 2001. The Imperial Hunter on Gupta Coins. *Numismatic Studies* 6, pp. 144-152.

Srivastava, Prashant 2004. *Art Motifs on Ancient Indian Coins*. New Delhi.

Srivastava, Prashant 2005. Two Śaka-Pahlava Kings Named Azes ? A K Sinha (ed), *Dimensions of Indian History* (Proceedings of the UP History Congress, 2003), (New Delhi, 2005), pp. 74-79.

Srivastava, Prashant 2007. *The Apracharajas* (A History based on Coins and Inscriptions). Delhi.

Srivastava, Prashant 2007. Greek Divinities on Śaka-Pahlava Coins. S P Shukla, *et al* (ed), *History and Heritage* (in Honour of Prof K K Thaplyal), (Delhi, 2007) 1, pp. 237-266.

Srivastava, Prashant 2007. The So-called 'Bhagamoya' Inscription of the Time of Vijayamitra, Azes Year 77. *Satata* 1, pp. 177-180.

Srivastava, Prashant 2008. Die-striking Mode of Fabrication of Coins : Its Origin in India, *Journal of the Numismatic Society of India* 70, pp. 28-31.

Stein, M Aurel 1888. Zoroastrian Deities on Indo-Scythian Coins. *Indian Antiquary* 17, pp. 89-98.

Stein, Aurel 1929. *Kharoshṭhī Inscriptions discovered by Sir A Stein in Chinese Turkestan*, 3 vols. Oxford.

Tarn, W W 1948. *Alexander the Great*, 2 vols. Cambridge.

Tarn, W W 1980. *The Greeks in Bactria and India*. Reprint, New Delhi.

Thaplyal, K K 2012. *The Imperial Guptas—A Political Study*. New Delhi.

Thaplyal, K K, and Prashant Srivastava 1998. *Coins of Ancient India*. Lucknow.

Vanaja, R 1983. *Indian Coinage*. New Delhi.

Wheeler, R E M 1954. *Rome Beyond the Imperial Frontiers*. London.

Whitehead, R B 1914. *Catalogue of the Coins in the Punjab Museum, Lahore* 1. The Indo-Greek Coins. Oxford.

Whitehead, R B 1922. *Pre-Mohammadan Coinage of North-West India*. Numismatic Notes and Monographs 13. New York.

Whitehead, R B 1923. Notes on Indo-Greek Numismatics. *Numismatic Chronicle*, pp. 294-343.

Whitehead, R B 1940. Notes on the Indo-Greeks, Part 1. *Numismatic Chronicle*, pp. 89-122.

Whitehead, R B 1943. The Eastern Satrap Sophytes. *Numismatic Chronicle* 1943, pp. 60-72.

Whitehead, R B 1947. Notes on the Indo-Greeks, Part 2. *Numismatic Chronicle*, pp. 28-51.

Whitehead, R B 1950. Notes on the Indo-Greeks, Part 3. *Numismatic Chronicle*, pp. 205-232.

Whitehead, R B 1975. Commentary on Rare and Unique Coins. J H Marshall, *Taxila* 2, pp. 830-842.

Wilkins, W J 2006. *Hindu Mythology : Vedic and Purāṇic*. Indian reprint, New Delhi.

Wilson, H H 1971. *Ariana Antiqua—A Descriptive Account of the Antiquities and Coins of Afghanistan*. Indian Reprint, Delhi.

Wroth, W 1903. *A Catalogue of the Greek Coins in the British Museum, London*. Coins of Parthia. London.

Zimmer, Heinrich 1999. *Myths and Symbols in Indian Art and Civilization*. Edited by Joseph Campbell. Indian reprint, Delhi.

Index

B

C

D

R

S

T

U

V

W

Y

Z

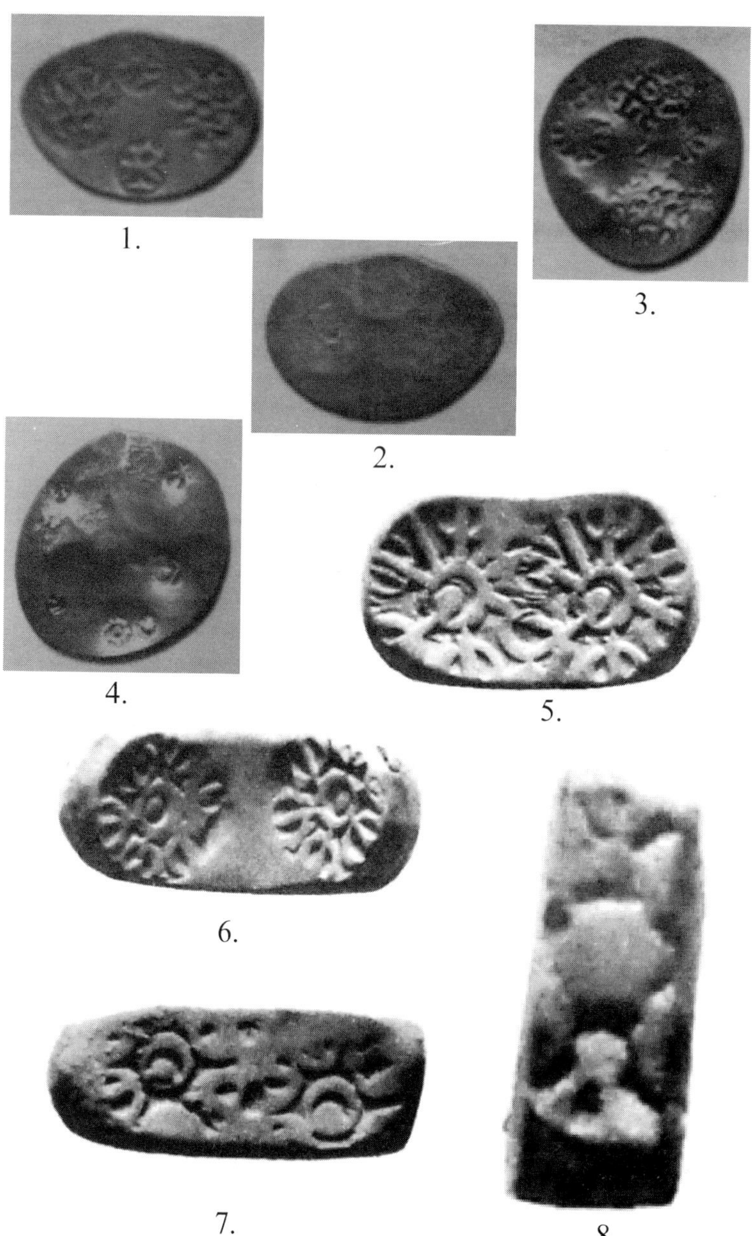

1.

2.

3.

4.

5.

6.

7.

8.

9.
10.
11.
12.
13.
14.
15.

16.

17.

18.

19.

20.

21.

22.

23.

24.

25.

26.

27.

28.

29.

30. 31. 32. 33. 34. 35. 36.

37. 38. 39. 40. 41. 42. 43.

44. 45. 46. 47. 48. 49. 50.

51.

52.

53.

54.

55.

56.

57.